# Building Next-Generation Software Solutions

*A Detailed Approach to Cross-Platform Programming with Python and C#*

THOMPSON CARTER

Table of Content

# *TABLE OF CONTENTS*

# *INTRODUCTION*

In today's fast-paced digital world, the demand for applications that can seamlessly run across multiple platforms has never been higher. From mobile phones and tablets to desktops, laptops, and even the web, users expect a consistent, reliable, and engaging experience regardless of the device or operating system they are using. As developers, the ability to create applications that meet these expectations—without duplicating effort or compromising on quality—has become a critical skill. This book, *"Building Next-Generation Software Solutions: A Detailed Approach to Cross-Platform Programming with Python and C#,"* is your comprehensive guide to understanding, implementing, and mastering cross-platform development.

The challenge of building cross-platform applications lies not only in writing code that works on different operating systems but also in navigating the complexities of platform-specific features, ensuring optimal performance, and providing a user-friendly experience across all environments. This book is designed to provide you with the tools, knowledge, and strategies to tackle these challenges effectively, specifically using two of the most powerful programming languages: **Python** and **C#**.

## Why Cross-Platform Development?

Traditionally, building software for multiple platforms meant writing different versions of the same application for each target operating system. This approach was not only time-consuming but also costly, especially when it came to maintenance and updates. The advent of **cross-platform frameworks** has revolutionized the development landscape by offering tools that allow developers to write a single codebase and deploy it across different platforms.

Cross-platform development has several key advantages:

- **Reduced Development Time and Costs**: Writing one codebase for multiple platforms drastically cuts down the development time and resources required to create separate applications for each platform.
- **Consistency in User Experience**: With cross-platform development, you can ensure that users enjoy a similar experience, whether they're using Android, iOS, Windows, macOS, or the web.
- **Easier Maintenance**: Instead of managing multiple codebases, cross-platform solutions allow you to maintain and update a single codebase, streamlining bug fixes and feature updates.

However, despite these advantages, cross-platform development still comes with its own set of challenges. Handling platform-specific requirements, optimizing performance, and ensuring that the app adheres to each platform's design guidelines are just a few of the hurdles developers face.

## The Power of Python and C# in Cross-Platform Development

Both **Python** and **C#** are dynamic, versatile languages that have carved out significant places in the software development world. Each brings unique strengths to cross-platform development.

- **Python**: Known for its simplicity and readability, Python has long been a go-to language for tasks such as web development, data science, automation, and scripting. With the rise of cross-platform frameworks like **Kivy**, **BeeWare**, and **PyQt**, Python has expanded its reach into mobile and desktop application development. Python's vibrant ecosystem of libraries, coupled with its ease of learning, makes it an excellent choice for developers looking to quickly prototype and build cross-platform applications.
- **C#**: C# has evolved significantly over the years and is now one of the most robust languages for building cross-platform applications, especially in the realm of mobile development. With the advent of **Xamarin** and **.NET MAUI**, C# has become a dominant force in creating high-performance, natively compiled applications for **Android**, **iOS**, **macOS**, **Windows**, and more. Its deep integration with the **Microsoft ecosystem**, along with the backing of **Azure** and **Visual Studio**, makes it an ideal choice for developers targeting enterprise applications or looking to take full advantage of the **.NET** platform.

This book will explore how to harness the power of both Python and C# to build effective, high-performance cross-platform applications, providing you with a well-rounded understanding of both languages and their respective ecosystems. Whether you are a developer with a Python background looking to expand your skills into mobile and desktop development or a C# developer looking to deepen your expertise in cross-platform solutions, this book will guide you through the necessary steps to master these technologies.

## What This Book Offers

This book is designed to be a practical, hands-on guide to cross-platform development with Python and C#. Throughout the chapters, we will explore both theoretical concepts and real-world case studies to give you the knowledge and tools needed to succeed in building cross-platform applications.

The book is divided into several parts:

1. **Introduction to Cross-Platform Development**: We begin with an overview of the landscape of cross-platform development, including the challenges, benefits, and tools available today. You will also get an introduction to the core concepts of cross-platform programming.
2. **Setting Up the Development Environment**: This section will guide you through setting up your environment for Python and C# cross-platform development. It covers the installation of key tools, frameworks, and IDEs like **Visual Studio**, **Xcode**, and **PyCharm** for Python, ensuring that you're ready to start developing right away.

3. **Core Principles of Cross-Platform Development**: Here, we dive deep into the principles that underpin cross-platform development, such as handling user interfaces, managing dependencies, and working with databases. We'll explore tools like **Kivy** for Python and **.NET MAUI** for C#, which allow you to create powerful cross-platform apps.

4. **Building Cross-Platform Applications**: We provide a detailed, step-by-step guide to building your own cross-platform applications using Python and C#. You'll learn how to create user interfaces, interact with device features like cameras and geolocation, and ensure your apps are optimized for all target platforms.

5. **Advanced Cross-Platform Concepts**: This part delves into more advanced topics, including concurrency, parallelism, testing strategies, and CI/CD pipelines. You'll learn how to optimize your app's performance and ensure its stability with robust testing and continuous deployment.

6. **Real-World Case Studies and Examples**: To solidify the concepts you've learned, we'll go through real-world case studies. These case studies will involve building a **cross-platform desktop application** and a **cross-platform mobile application**, using Python and C# in parallel to highlight the strengths and challenges of each language.

7. **Future Trends in Cross-Platform Development**: The final part of the book looks at the future of cross-platform development. We'll explore emerging

trends, such as **WebAssembly, serverless computing**, and the evolution of **Flutter, React Native**, and **.NET MAUI**, and how both Python and C# are adapting to meet these new challenges.

## Who This Book is For

This book is ideal for developers who want to expand their skills and dive into the world of cross-platform application development. Whether you're a seasoned Python developer who wants to explore mobile and desktop application development, a C# developer eager to harness the power of **.NET MAUI**, or even a beginner looking for a clear and comprehensive guide to get started with cross-platform development, this book is for you.

The book assumes a basic understanding of programming concepts. While familiarity with Python and C# is beneficial, it is not required, as the book will introduce you to the necessary tools and frameworks step by step.

## Why Choose Python and C# for Cross-Platform Development?

Both **Python** and **C#** have unique advantages that make them excellent choices for cross-platform development:

- **Python**:
    - Easy to learn and use, with a large, active community.
    - Great for rapid prototyping and small to medium-sized applications.

o Extensive libraries and frameworks for everything from data science to web and mobile development.

- **C#:**
  o Strong performance and integration with Microsoft's ecosystem.
  o Powerful cross-platform frameworks like **Xamarin** and **.NET MAUI.**
  o Excellent tools for building enterprise-grade, high-performance applications.

By mastering both languages in the context of cross-platform development, you will be well-equipped to tackle any project, whether you're building a mobile app for iOS and Android, a desktop app for Windows and macOS, or even a web app that works across all devices.

## Conclusion

Cross-platform development is the future of software development, and the tools and languages you choose to work with will shape the success of your applications. This book is designed to equip you with the knowledge and hands-on experience to build powerful, efficient, and cross-platform applications using **Python** and **C#**. By the end of this journey, you will have the skills necessary to create applications that meet the demands of modern users, delivering seamless experiences across all platforms

# CHAPTER 1

# INTRODUCTION TO SOFTWARE DEVELOPMENT

*Overview of the Software Development Landscape*

The field of software development has undergone significant changes over the decades. In the early days of computing, software was tightly bound to the hardware it was designed for. Developers wrote applications specifically for a single machine or platform, often resulting in applications that couldn't run on different devices or operating systems.

However, as technology advanced, so did the need for software to work on multiple platforms. The rise of personal computers, mobile devices, and various operating systems like Windows, macOS, and Linux led to the introduction of more sophisticated software development practices. The Internet and cloud technologies further expanded the complexity of building software that works across different devices and environments.

Today, the software development landscape is diverse and multi-faceted, involving applications for desktop, mobile, web, and even embedded systems. To navigate this landscape, developers use a variety of languages, frameworks, and tools to create applications that are functional, efficient, and user-friendly.

13

*The Evolution of Software Development*

- **Early Days of Programming:** In the early years of programming, the software was written in machine language or assembly, directly interacting with hardware. The applications were highly specific to the platform they were built for, with little to no cross-platform compatibility.
- **Introduction of High-Level Languages:** High-level programming languages such as C and Java brought more flexibility, enabling developers to write code that could run on multiple platforms, though it still required platform-specific adjustments.
- **The Rise of Object-Oriented Programming (OOP):** Object-Oriented Programming (OOP) principles, introduced in the 1980s, helped developers create reusable and maintainable code. While OOP didn't directly address cross-platform compatibility, it laid the groundwork for creating more modular applications that could eventually be adapted across platforms.
- **Cross-Platform Frameworks and Tools:** The 2000s saw the development of more robust cross-platform frameworks and libraries such as Java's "Write Once, Run Anywhere" mantra, and tools like Qt and Mono that enabled developers to write code that could be easily ported across different systems.
- **Web and Mobile Development:** The rise of mobile computing and the internet in the 2010s brought forward the necessity of building applications that could run on web browsers, mobile devices, and

desktops alike. Technologies like HTML5, CSS3, JavaScript, and later frameworks such as React and Angular, allowed developers to write applications that could run in any modern browser.

- **Modern Cross-Platform Solutions:** Today, with the advent of tools like Xamarin, Flutter, React Native, and progressive web apps, developers have a broader range of frameworks that allow them to write code once and deploy it across multiple platforms. The ability to develop cross-platform apps with tools that support Android, iOS, Windows, and even macOS has made it easier to reach global audiences with a single codebase.

*Why Cross-Platform Programming is Important*

In today's fast-paced digital world, businesses and developers face increasing pressure to build software that works across multiple platforms. Cross-platform programming addresses this need by allowing developers to create applications that can run on various operating systems, devices, and environments without having to write separate code for each one.

**Key Benefits of Cross-Platform Programming:**

1. **Cost Efficiency:** Writing separate code for each platform (e.g., iOS, Android, Windows) can be time-consuming and expensive. With cross-platform development, developers can use the same codebase for different platforms, saving both time and money.

2. **Faster Time-to-Market:** By reusing the same code across platforms, developers can deliver software faster. This is especially important in competitive markets where the speed at which a product reaches consumers can make a significant difference.

3. **Wider Reach:** A cross-platform approach allows applications to be deployed on a variety of devices and operating systems, increasing the potential user base.

4. **Consistency and Maintenance:** Maintaining a single codebase is much easier than managing multiple versions of the same software for different platforms. This also ensures consistent functionality and user experience across platforms.

5. **Leveraging Community and Framework Support:** With cross-platform tools like Python, C#, and various frameworks, developers can tap into a large community and extensive library of resources. This speeds up development and troubleshooting.

6. **Future-Proofing:** As technology continues to evolve, cross-platform development enables software to remain adaptable to new devices and platforms, reducing the need for constant redevelopment.

*The Challenges of Cross-Platform Development*

While there are many benefits to cross-platform programming, it's not without its challenges:

- **Platform-Specific Features:** Certain platform-specific features may require custom solutions or

16

compromises when developing cross-platform apps. Accessing hardware or utilizing operating system-specific functionalities can sometimes be tricky.

- **Performance Issues:** Cross-platform frameworks often introduce an additional layer of abstraction, which can impact performance. Native applications tend to be faster because they can take full advantage of platform-specific optimizations.

- **Complexity of Testing:** Testing cross-platform applications requires running the software on various platforms to ensure it works as expected everywhere. This can be more time-consuming than testing a native application.

- **Limited Access to Native UI Components:** Cross-platform frameworks may not offer the same level of access to native UI components as platform-specific development tools, which can impact the user experience.

Despite these challenges, the continued evolution of cross-platform tools and frameworks is making it increasingly feasible to build high-quality, performant applications across multiple platforms.

By the end of this chapter, readers should have a clear understanding of the software development landscape, the evolution of programming practices, and why cross-platform programming has become essential in the modern development world.

# CHAPTER 2

# *UNDERSTANDING CROSS-PLATFORM DEVELOPMENT*

*What is Cross-Platform Development?*

Cross-platform development refers to the practice of building software applications that can run on multiple operating systems and devices without requiring significant changes to the underlying codebase. The goal is to create a single version of the application that works seamlessly across a variety of platforms, including desktop, mobile, and web environments.

In a cross-platform approach, developers write code once and use frameworks or tools to deploy it to multiple platforms. This eliminates the need to develop separate versions of the same application for each platform, such as Android, iOS, Windows, and macOS.

The concept of cross-platform development has grown in popularity due to the diverse landscape of devices and operating systems, ranging from smartphones and tablets to desktops, wearables, and even embedded systems. Users now expect applications to be available on all their devices, regardless of the platform they are using.

*Key Characteristics of Cross-Platform Development*

1. **Single Codebase**: One of the defining features of cross-platform development is the use of a single codebase that can be deployed to multiple platforms. This means developers write the application once and adapt it to work across different environments.

2. **Platform Independence**: Cross-platform tools enable applications to run on a variety of platforms without needing significant code changes. The focus is on minimizing platform-specific code while maximizing code reuse.

3. **Code Translation or Abstraction**: Most cross-platform frameworks work by translating or abstracting platform-specific code into a format that is compatible with other operating systems. This often involves using APIs, wrappers, or containerized environments to bridge the gap between platforms.

*Challenges of Cross-Platform Development*

While cross-platform development provides significant benefits, it comes with its own set of challenges:

1. **Performance Issues**: Cross-platform frameworks often introduce an additional layer of abstraction between the application and the operating system. This can result in lower performance compared to native applications, which are built specifically for one platform. The app might not perform as well,

especially when it comes to graphics-intensive operations or accessing hardware-specific features.

2. **Platform-Specific Features**: Some platforms offer unique features, APIs, or hardware access that cannot be fully utilized using cross-platform tools. Developers may encounter limitations when trying to integrate these features into a cross-platform application. For example, utilizing platform-specific gestures on mobile devices or system-level functionalities may require additional customization.

3. **User Interface (UI) Consistency**: Cross-platform development tools strive to create a consistent look and feel across platforms, but native user interface elements on different platforms can vary significantly. Ensuring that the app's UI provides a seamless and intuitive experience on all platforms without compromising the native design guidelines can be a challenge.

4. **Fragmentation**: With many different versions of operating systems and devices in use, developers must ensure their applications are compatible across a wide range of devices. This fragmentation can increase the complexity of development, testing, and maintenance.

5. **Limited Access to Native Libraries**: Cross-platform frameworks often provide abstractions for interacting with native libraries. However, this abstraction can sometimes limit access to more specialized libraries or features offered by the native platform, forcing developers to write custom

solutions or use platform-specific tools for some functionalities.

*Benefits of Cross-Platform Development*

Despite the challenges, cross-platform development offers numerous advantages that make it an attractive approach for modern software development:

1. **Cost-Effectiveness**: One of the most significant advantages of cross-platform development is cost savings. By maintaining a single codebase, developers can eliminate the need to write and maintain separate code for multiple platforms. This reduces development time, the number of developers required, and associated costs.

2. **Faster Time-to-Market**: With cross-platform development, businesses can release applications to multiple platforms simultaneously. This faster deployment is essential in competitive markets where getting products to users quickly can be a key differentiator.

3. **Wider Reach**: By developing applications for multiple platforms, companies can reach a broader audience. Cross-platform development allows developers to target mobile, desktop, and web users with a single application, extending its reach to a variety of device types.

4. **Easier Maintenance and Updates**: Maintaining a single codebase is much more efficient than managing separate codebases for each platform. Bug fixes, updates, and new features can be rolled out to

all platforms simultaneously, making ongoing maintenance more straightforward.

5. **Consistency Across Platforms**: Cross-platform development ensures that users have a consistent experience regardless of the platform they use. The core functionality of the application will be the same across all devices, which helps improve the overall user experience.

6. **Reusability of Code**: One of the most significant advantages of cross-platform development is the ability to reuse code across platforms. A large portion of the application logic and business code can be shared, reducing the amount of work required to develop applications for multiple environments.

*Tools and Frameworks Available for Cross-Platform Development*

The evolution of cross-platform development has been driven by the creation of powerful tools and frameworks that allow developers to build applications that run across multiple platforms. Some of the most popular cross-platform development tools include:

1. **Xamarin**
   Xamarin is a cross-platform development framework based on C# and .NET. It allows developers to write applications for Android, iOS, and Windows using a single codebase. Xamarin compiles the application into native code for each platform, offering better performance than some other frameworks.

2. **Flutter**
   Developed by Google, Flutter is a UI toolkit for

22

building natively compiled applications for mobile, web, and desktop from a single codebase. Flutter uses the Dart programming language and allows developers to create high-performance applications with beautiful UIs that closely resemble native experiences.

3. **React**                              **Native**

   React Native is a popular framework for building mobile applications using JavaScript and React. With React Native, developers can write applications for iOS and Android using a single codebase. It provides near-native performance and allows developers to use native components when needed.

4. **Apache**            **Cordova**           **(PhoneGap)**

   Apache Cordova is an open-source platform for building mobile applications using HTML, CSS, and JavaScript. It enables developers to create applications that can run on multiple mobile platforms, including iOS, Android, and Windows Phone.

5. **Qt**

   Qt is a cross-platform development framework that allows developers to build applications for desktop and embedded devices. It provides a wide range of tools and libraries for building high-performance applications with native-like UIs.

6. **JavaFX**

   JavaFX is a framework for building cross-platform desktop applications. It allows developers to create rich UIs and provides a wide range of APIs for developing applications that run on Windows, macOS, and Linux.

7. **Electron**

   Electron is a framework that allows developers to build cross-platform desktop applications using web technologies such as HTML, CSS, and JavaScript. Applications built with Electron can run on Windows, macOS, and Linux, and popular apps like Visual Studio Code and Slack are built with Electron.

8. **Mono**

   Mono is an open-source implementation of the .NET framework that allows developers to create cross-platform applications using C# and .NET technologies. It supports Windows, Linux, macOS, and other platforms.

9. **Unity**

   Unity is primarily a game development engine, but it also supports the creation of interactive 3D applications and simulations for multiple platforms, including desktop, mobile, and consoles. It allows developers to write applications once and deploy them across a variety of platforms.

---

By the end of this chapter, readers should have a comprehensive understanding of cross-platform development, its benefits and challenges, and the tools available to help developers create cross-platform applications. This foundation will set the stage for diving deeper into building practical, cross-platform solutions with Python and C# in the following chapters.

# CHAPTER 3

# THE ROLE OF PYTHON IN CROSS-PLATFORM DEVELOPMENT

*Exploring Python's Versatility*

Python is often hailed as one of the most versatile and beginner-friendly programming languages in the world. Its simplicity, readability, and broad ecosystem make it an excellent choice for a variety of software development tasks, including cross-platform development.

While Python's primary strength lies in its use for backend development, data science, web development, and automation, its role in cross-platform development is equally significant. Thanks to its portability, large number of libraries, and an active community, Python can be leveraged to create applications that run seamlessly across multiple platforms, from desktops and mobile devices to the web and embedded systems.

One of Python's standout features is that it is an interpreted language, meaning that the same code can often run on different platforms without modification, as long as the Python interpreter is available. This feature makes it an ideal candidate for cross-platform applications, where developers do not want to invest significant effort into platform-specific development.

*Strengths of Python in Cross-Platform Development*

1. **Simplicity        and        Readability**
   Python is designed to be intuitive and easy to read, which allows developers to write code faster and with fewer errors. The clear and concise syntax, combined with excellent documentation and community support, makes Python an attractive choice for developers, especially when building cross-platform solutions where quick development cycles are essential.

2. **Wide Range of Libraries and Frameworks**
   Python boasts an extensive collection of libraries and frameworks that support cross-platform development. Some of the popular libraries that facilitate building cross-platform applications include:
   - **Kivy**: An open-source Python library for developing multitouch applications, Kivy is well-suited for building cross-platform mobile apps and desktop applications.
   - **BeeWare**: BeeWare is a collection of tools for building Python applications that run on iOS, Android, macOS, Linux, and Windows. It allows developers to write a single codebase that works across a wide range of platforms.
   - **PyQt / PySide**: These libraries provide bindings to the Qt application framework, enabling the creation of cross-platform graphical user interfaces (GUIs) for desktop applications.

26

o **Flask / Django**: While Flask and Django are primarily web frameworks, they help in developing cross-platform web applications that can be accessed from any device with a web browser.

3. **Portability**
Python applications are highly portable, which is a significant advantage for cross-platform development. Python is supported on all major operating systems, including Windows, macOS, and Linux. As long as the end-user has a Python interpreter installed, the same Python code can be executed across platforms with minimal changes.

4. **Integration with Other Languages**
Python integrates well with other programming languages, which can be beneficial in cross-platform development. For example, if performance-critical code needs to be written, Python allows easy integration with C, C++, and Java. This is especially useful in cases where certain platform-specific optimizations or integrations are needed.

5. **Cross-Platform GUI Frameworks**
Python's ability to create graphical user interfaces (GUIs) that work across different operating systems is another reason it's a popular choice for cross-platform development. Frameworks like Kivy, Tkinter, and PyQt enable developers to create applications with native-looking interfaces that work seamlessly on Windows, macOS, and Linux. Some Python frameworks, such as PyQt and wxPython, even allow for creating applications with custom widgets that are consistent across different platforms.

27

6. **Rapid Prototyping and Development**
Python's concise syntax and large selection of libraries for rapid application development (RAD) allow developers to quickly prototype and iterate on cross-platform applications. The high-level nature of Python, combined with its rich ecosystem, makes it ideal for testing ideas quickly before transitioning to more complex, performance-optimized solutions.

*Why Python is a Go-To Choice for Developers*

Python's role in cross-platform development is growing steadily, and here's why developers often choose it for building universal applications:

1. **Community Support and Resources**
One of Python's biggest strengths is its active and vibrant community. With millions of developers around the world, there is no shortage of resources, from documentation and tutorials to forums and open-source projects. This extensive community support makes it easier for developers to overcome challenges, share knowledge, and collaborate on projects.

2. **Cross-Platform Mobile Development**
Python can be used for developing cross-platform mobile apps with tools like Kivy, BeeWare, and PyQt. These frameworks allow Python developers to write mobile applications that work on both Android and iOS. While Python may not have the same native performance as languages like Java or Swift, it offers

the advantage of a unified codebase that works on multiple platforms, including mobile.

3. **Cross-Platform Web Applications**
   Python is also an excellent choice for developing cross-platform web applications. Popular web frameworks like Django and Flask enable developers to build powerful web applications that work across all platforms via web browsers. These frameworks follow best practices and provide tools for rapid development while ensuring that the application remains scalable and maintainable.

4. **Integration with Cloud and IoT**
   As cloud computing and the Internet of Things (IoT) have gained prominence, Python has proven itself to be an essential language for building cross-platform cloud-based solutions. Python's integration with various cloud platforms, including AWS, Google Cloud, and Microsoft Azure, allows developers to create cross-platform applications that interact with cloud services. Additionally, Python can be used to develop applications for IoT devices, which often need to work across various platforms and hardware configurations.

5. **Cross-Platform Automation**
   Python is widely used for writing automation scripts, and its cross-platform nature allows these scripts to run seamlessly across different systems. Whether it's automating server management, data pipelines, or software testing, Python's simplicity and extensive libraries make it a preferred tool for automating tasks across different platforms.

6. **Rich Ecosystem for Data and Machine Learning**
   While not directly related to traditional cross-platform applications, Python's strong presence in fields like data science, artificial intelligence, and machine learning cannot be overlooked. Libraries like TensorFlow, PyTorch, and scikit-learn allow developers to create AI-powered cross-platform applications. Whether it's for desktop, web, or mobile, Python can be the language of choice when integrating advanced data processing and machine learning features into cross-platform applications.

7. **Open          Source          and          Free**
   Python is open-source and free to use, which means that developers can access it without worrying about licensing fees. This makes it an appealing option for startups, open-source projects, and small businesses that need to develop cross-platform software but may have limited budgets.

*Popular Python Tools for Cross-Platform Development*

1. **PyInstaller**
   PyInstaller is a tool that allows developers to bundle Python applications into standalone executables that can run on Windows, macOS, and Linux. This is useful when you need to distribute a Python application to end-users who might not have Python installed.

2. **cx_Freeze**
   cx_Freeze is another tool for packaging Python applications into standalone executables. It supports

Windows, macOS, and Linux and is commonly used for creating cross-platform desktop applications.

3. **Docker**

   Docker allows developers to containerize applications, making it easy to develop, test, and deploy cross-platform applications. It ensures that Python applications run consistently across different environments by packaging them with all their dependencies into containers.

4. **Anaconda**

   Anaconda is a distribution of Python and R for data science and scientific computing. It simplifies the process of setting up a cross-platform development environment by managing packages, environments, and dependencies.

---

*Conclusion*

Python's versatility, extensive libraries, ease of use, and broad platform support make it a compelling choice for cross-platform development. Whether you're developing mobile applications, desktop software, or web applications, Python provides the flexibility and power needed to create high-quality, cross-platform solutions. Its ability to integrate seamlessly with other technologies further strengthens its role in modern software development, making it one of the go-to languages for developers looking to build universal applications.

# CHAPTER 4

# THE POWER OF C# FOR CROSS-PLATFORM SOLUTIONS

*Understanding C#'s Role in Modern Software Development*

C# (pronounced "C-sharp") is a high-level, object-oriented programming language developed by Microsoft. Initially introduced as a core language for Windows applications, C# has evolved into a versatile tool for building applications across a variety of platforms. Its design is heavily influenced by C++, Java, and other programming languages, making it both powerful and accessible to developers familiar with modern software design paradigms.

C# is a key component of the .NET ecosystem, which includes the .NET Framework, .NET Core, and Xamarin. Over the years, C# has transformed from a Windows-centric language into a multi-purpose language capable of building applications for a broad range of environments, including mobile devices, cloud services, and web applications. The rise of .NET Core and Xamarin has been instrumental in making C# a go-to language for cross-platform development.

*C# and the .NET Ecosystem*

The .NET ecosystem is at the heart of C#'s cross-platform capabilities. The introduction of .NET Core, a cross-platform version of the .NET Framework, marked a pivotal moment in the evolution of C#. .NET Core enables developers to build and run applications on a variety of platforms, including Windows, macOS, and Linux, without being tied to the limitations of the traditional .NET Framework.

1. **.NET**      **Core**

    .NET Core is a lightweight, modular, open-source platform that supports cross-platform development. Unlike the .NET Framework, which was Windows-specific, .NET Core was built from the ground up to be platform-agnostic. Developers can write C# applications in .NET Core that can run on Linux, macOS, and Windows, expanding C#'s reach far beyond its initial Windows-focused ecosystem.

    Key advantages of .NET Core for cross-platform development include:

    - o **Performance:** .NET Core is optimized for high-performance applications, making it suitable for everything from web servers to high-throughput data processing.
    - o **Modular Design:** .NET Core's modular structure allows developers to include only the necessary libraries, which leads to smaller application sizes and better resource management.
    - o **Cross-Platform Support:** .NET Core allows developers to write C# code once and run it on multiple platforms, eliminating the need to rewrite the code for each operating system.

- o **Unified Development:** With .NET Core, developers can build various types of applications—console, web, mobile, cloud, and more—using the same language and runtime environment.

2. **ASP.NET                                    Core**

   ASP.NET Core, a framework built on top of .NET Core, enables the development of high-performance, scalable web applications. It allows developers to build web applications that run on any platform, with support for everything from APIs to complex web front-ends. ASP.NET Core is cross-platform by nature and provides a unified way to build both back-end and front-end web applications using C#.

3. **Entity           Framework           Core**

   Entity Framework Core is an Object-Relational Mapping (ORM) framework that simplifies data access in .NET Core applications. It enables developers to write cross-platform database applications without worrying about underlying platform-specific database access mechanisms.

*The Role of Xamarin in Cross-Platform Mobile Development*

Xamarin is a framework developed by Microsoft that allows developers to build cross-platform mobile applications using C#. Xamarin enables developers to write mobile applications for both Android and iOS using a shared C# codebase. Xamarin leverages the .NET ecosystem to provide a rich set of libraries, APIs, and tools for building performant mobile applications that behave like native apps on both platforms.

34

Xamarin offers several key features that make it a popular choice for cross-platform mobile development:

1. **Single Codebase for iOS and Android**
   One of the standout features of Xamarin is the ability to write a single codebase that targets both Android and iOS. This reduces development time, increases productivity, and ensures that the application's core logic remains consistent across both platforms.

2. **Native Performance**
   Xamarin compiles code to native ARM code, which allows for high-performance applications. The resulting apps run natively on Android and iOS devices, ensuring that performance is on par with apps written in platform-specific languages like Java or Swift.

3. **Access to Native APIs**
   Xamarin provides full access to platform-specific APIs, allowing developers to tap into native device features like cameras, geolocation, and accelerometers. This enables the development of highly interactive and feature-rich applications that utilize the full capabilities of the target devices.

4. **Xamarin.Forms**
   Xamarin.Forms is a UI toolkit that allows developers to build a single user interface that works across both Android and iOS. While Xamarin.Forms doesn't always offer the level of customization and control that Xamarin's native APIs provide, it's an excellent choice for building simpler mobile applications that need to run on both platforms without extensive platform-specific customization.

5. **Integration with Visual Studio**
Xamarin integrates seamlessly with Microsoft Visual Studio, one of the most powerful IDEs available for C# development. Visual Studio offers robust debugging tools, UI designers, and testing frameworks, which simplify the mobile development process and speed up development cycles.

*The Advantages of Using C# for Cross-Platform Development*

1. **Unified Language for All Platforms**
One of the biggest benefits of using C# for cross-platform development is the ability to use a single language across all types of applications. Whether you're building a web application with ASP.NET Core, a mobile app with Xamarin, or a desktop application with .NET Core, C# remains the language of choice. This unified approach reduces the learning curve and allows developers to be more efficient when working on different types of projects.

2. **Code Reusability and Maintainability**
C# promotes code reusability through features like object-oriented programming (OOP), which makes it easier to maintain and extend cross-platform applications. With tools like Xamarin and .NET Core, a large portion of the codebase can be shared across platforms, making updates and bug fixes more efficient.

3. **Microsoft Support and Ecosystem**
As a language developed and maintained by Microsoft, C# benefits from continuous updates, support, and integration with other Microsoft tools

and services. Developers using C# for cross-platform solutions can take advantage of a wide range of Microsoft technologies, such as Azure for cloud computing, Visual Studio for development, and Power BI for data analytics.

4. **Rich Library Ecosystem**
   The .NET ecosystem provides a rich collection of libraries and frameworks, from data access tools (Entity Framework Core) to UI development (Xamarin.Forms), making it easy for developers to find pre-built components for almost any task. This significantly speeds up the development process and allows developers to focus on the core features of their applications.

5. **Strong Community and Documentation**
   C# has a vast, active community of developers and extensive documentation. Whether you need support for a specific platform or a detailed guide on using a particular library, the C# ecosystem has a wealth of resources available. This community-driven approach helps ensure that C# remains relevant and well-supported for years to come.

6. **Cross-Platform for Desktop, Mobile, Web, and Cloud**
   With Xamarin for mobile, .NET Core for desktop applications, ASP.NET Core for web development, and Azure for cloud-based solutions, C# has become a truly cross-platform language. Developers can build full-stack applications using C# that target multiple environments, simplifying both development and deployment processes.

*Challenges of Using C# for Cross-Platform Development*

1. **Learning Curve for New Developers**
   While C# is known for its simplicity, newcomers to the language or the .NET ecosystem might face a learning curve, especially when trying to navigate the nuances of cross-platform development. Understanding the differences between Xamarin, .NET Core, and other components may take time.

2. **Platform-Specific Customization**
   Although Xamarin and .NET Core allow for a shared codebase, there may still be cases where platform-specific customization is necessary. This can involve writing platform-dependent code, which can sometimes negate the benefits of using a single codebase.

3. **Limited Support for Some Features**
   While Xamarin and .NET Core offer a wide array of features, there are some platform-specific features or customizations that may not be fully supported, particularly on newer operating systems or specialized devices.

---

*Conclusion*

C# has established itself as a powerhouse for cross-platform development, thanks to its integration with the .NET ecosystem and the rise of tools like Xamarin. The ability to use a single language across mobile, web, desktop, and cloud environments has made C# a popular choice for developers who want to build universal applications. While there are challenges to be mindful of, the numerous advantages C# offers, including performance, code reusability, and extensive support, make it a go-to language for modern cross-platform solutions.

# CHAPTER 5

# COMPARING PYTHON AND C#: A LANGUAGE SHOWDOWN

*Introduction*

Both Python and C# are powerful, widely-used programming languages that have gained immense popularity in the world of software development. When it comes to cross-platform development, each language has its own strengths and weaknesses, and they cater to different types of use cases. While Python is renowned for its simplicity, ease of learning, and versatility, C# stands out with its strong ties to the .NET ecosystem and its robust support for enterprise-level applications. In this chapter, we'll explore a detailed comparison of Python and C# for cross-platform development, highlighting their strengths, weaknesses, and ideal use cases.

*Core Language Features*
Python: Simplicity and Flexibility

- **Syntax and Readability:** Python is known for its clean and easy-to-read syntax, which allows developers to write code quickly and intuitively. The language's minimalistic approach makes it a great choice for beginners and seasoned developers alike. Python's readability is often emphasized as one of its most attractive features, leading to faster development cycles and easier code maintenance.

- **Dynamically Typed:** Python is dynamically typed, which means variables are not explicitly declared with types. This can make development faster, but also potentially more error-prone, as type mismatches can lead to runtime errors.

- **Interpretation:** Python code is typically interpreted, meaning that it is executed line-by-line by the interpreter. While this makes it more flexible and easy to debug, it can lead to slower performance compared to compiled languages like C#.

## C#: Strong Typing and Performance

- **Syntax and Structure:** C# follows a more rigid and structured approach, borrowing heavily from languages like Java and C++. The language is statically typed, requiring the explicit declaration of variable types. This leads to safer and more predictable code, but can result in longer development times as developers have to be more specific in their code.

- **Compiled Language:** C# is a compiled language, meaning the code is first compiled into Intermediate Language (IL) and then executed by the .NET runtime (CLR). This provides a performance boost over interpreted languages like Python, as the code is optimized ahead of time. Additionally, the compiled nature makes C# suitable for performance-critical applications.

41

- **Object-Oriented Programming (OOP):** C# is fully object-oriented, meaning everything in the language is treated as an object. This allows for more organized, modular, and reusable code, which is particularly useful in large-scale projects.

*Cross-Platform Development*

Python for Cross-Platform Development

- **Portability:** Python's core feature is its portability. Python code is generally written once and can be run on various platforms (Windows, Linux, macOS) without modification, as long as the correct Python interpreter is installed. Python's cross-platform compatibility is one of the reasons it's so popular for rapid development and prototyping.
- **Frameworks for Cross-Platform Development:**
  - **Kivy:** A Python framework used for building cross-platform mobile apps and graphical applications. It supports both Android and iOS, as well as desktops.
  - **BeeWare:** A set of tools for building cross-platform applications, including mobile (iOS and Android) and desktop (Windows, macOS, and Linux) apps. BeeWare allows Python developers to write native user interfaces.
  - **PyQt / PySide:** Libraries that provide bindings to the Qt framework, enabling the creation of cross-platform desktop applications with native UIs.
- **Challenges:** While Python is highly portable, performance can be an issue for more resource-intensive applications. Python is slower than C# due to its interpreted nature, which can be a drawback

42

when building performance-critical cross-platform applications.

## C# for Cross-Platform Development

- **.NET Core and Xamarin:** The introduction of .NET Core (and its predecessor, Mono) has made C# a strong contender for cross-platform development. .NET Core allows C# applications to run on Windows, macOS, and Linux. Xamarin, a C#-based framework, is widely used for building cross-platform mobile applications for both Android and iOS using a shared C# codebase.
- **Frameworks for Cross-Platform Development:**
  - **Xamarin:** Xamarin allows developers to write cross-platform mobile applications with C# that target Android and iOS. It provides direct access to platform-specific APIs, ensuring that the applications behave natively on each platform.
  - **.NET MAUI (Multi-platform App UI):** A new cross-platform framework from Microsoft that extends Xamarin and allows developers to write cross-platform apps for Android, iOS, macOS, and Windows with a single codebase. It simplifies UI development and makes it easier to build applications that work on multiple platforms.
- **Performance:** One of the biggest advantages of C# in cross-platform development is performance. C# applications are compiled, which allows them to run much faster than Python applications, particularly in graphics-intensive applications like games or high-performance mobile apps.

43

*Use Cases and Ideal Applications*
Python Use Cases

- **Data Science and Machine Learning:** Python's simplicity, along with its rich ecosystem of libraries (such as TensorFlow, scikit-learn, and pandas), makes it the go-to language for data science, artificial intelligence, and machine learning. Its ability to quickly iterate on algorithms and prototypes makes it ideal for rapid experimentation.
- **Web Development:** Python has a strong presence in web development, with frameworks like Django and Flask making it easy to build web applications that run on any platform. These frameworks allow for the creation of scalable, secure, and feature-rich web applications that can be deployed on cloud platforms.
- **Automation and Scripting:** Python is widely used for automation tasks, from web scraping to automating repetitive system tasks. Its rich set of libraries makes it an excellent choice for writing scripts that can run on various operating systems.
- **Cross-Platform Desktop and Mobile Apps:** While not as common as other use cases, Python can be used to build simple desktop and mobile applications. However, it may not be the best choice for performance-heavy applications like games or complex native mobile apps.

C# Use Cases

- **Enterprise Applications:** C# is heavily used in building large-scale, enterprise-level applications

44

due to its strong object-oriented features, performance, and the integration with the .NET ecosystem. It is particularly suited for businesses that require secure, scalable, and maintainable applications.

- **Cross-Platform Mobile Apps:** Xamarin makes C# an excellent choice for mobile development, allowing developers to build cross-platform mobile applications that behave like native apps on both Android and iOS. Xamarin allows for maximum code reuse and easy access to device APIs, making it a popular choice for mobile app development.

- **Games Development:** C# is widely used in game development, especially with the Unity game engine. Unity is one of the most popular game development engines, and C# is its primary language for writing game logic. Developers can create games that run on multiple platforms, including Windows, macOS, iOS, Android, and consoles.

- **Web Development with ASP.NET Core:** ASP.NET Core, a framework built on top of .NET Core, allows developers to build fast, secure, and scalable web applications. With the ability to run on multiple platforms, ASP.NET Core is often used for building modern web applications and APIs.

*Strengths and Weaknesses Comparison*

| Feature | Python | C# |
|---|---|---|
| **Syntax and Learning Curve** | Simple, readable, great for beginners | More structured, higher learning curve |

| Feature | Python | C# |
| --- | --- | --- |
| Performance | Slower due to being interpreted | Faster due to being compiled |
| Cross-Platform Support | Highly portable with frameworks like Kivy, BeeWare | Strong support with .NET Core, Xamarin, .NET MAUI |
| Web Development | Excellent with frameworks like Django, Flask | Great with ASP.NET Core |
| Mobile Development | Limited, but can be done with Kivy, BeeWare | Excellent with Xamarin and .NET MAUI |
| Game Development | Not ideal for performance-heavy games | Strong in game development with Unity |
| Community and Ecosystem | Large community, rich in libraries | Strong Microsoft-backed ecosystem |
| Enterprise Solutions | Good for smaller to medium-sized applications | Excellent for large-scale enterprise apps |

*Conclusion*

Both Python and C# are excellent choices for cross-platform development, but their strengths and ideal use cases differ. Python excels in rapid development, data science, automation, and web development, making it an ideal choice for many use cases that require flexibility and speed. However, when it comes to performance-critical applications, especially in mobile and game development, C# offers superior performance, particularly with frameworks like Xamarin and .NET Core.

The decision between Python and C# ultimately depends on the specific project requirements. Python's ease of use and rapid prototyping capabilities make it ideal for small to medium-sized projects, data-heavy applications, and web applications, while C#'s performance, scalability, and strong enterprise support make it the go-to choice for large-scale, cross-platform applications that demand high performance.

## CHAPTER 6

# INSTALLING AND CONFIGURING PYTHON FOR CROSS-PLATFORM DEVELOPMENT

In this chapter, we'll walk through the steps to install and configure Python for cross-platform development. Python's portability across different platforms makes it an excellent choice for developing cross-platform applications, but setting up the environment correctly is crucial for ensuring smooth development. We'll cover the installation of Python itself, setting up development environments, and the essential tools and frameworks that make Python ideal for cross-platform development.

*Step 1: Installing Python on Different Platforms*

Python is supported on all major operating systems, including Windows, macOS, and Linux. Below are the steps for installing Python on each of these platforms.

Installing Python on Windows

1. **Download Python:**
    o Visit the official Python website.
    o Click on the "Download Python" button. The website will automatically detect the best version for your system.

2. **Run the Installer:**
   - o Launch the installer after downloading.
   - o **Important:** Make sure to check the option **"Add Python to PATH"** during the installation process. This ensures that you can run Python from the command line without needing to specify the installation path.

3. **Verify Installation:**
   - o Open a new command prompt window (search for `cmd`).
   - o Type the command `python --version` or `python3 --version` to verify the installation.
   - o If installed successfully, you'll see Python's version number.

Installing Python on macOS

1. **Download Python:**
   - o Visit the official Python website.
   - o Click on the "Download Python" button for macOS.

2. **Run the Installer:**
   - o Open the `.pkg` installer file once it has been downloaded.
   - o Follow the on-screen instructions to complete the installation.

3. **Verify Installation:**
   - o Open the Terminal (you can search for "Terminal" in Spotlight).
   - o Type `python3 --version` to check that Python is installed properly.

Installing Python on Linux

Python is often pre-installed on most Linux distributions, but if you need to install or update it, you can follow these steps:

1. **Using a Package Manager (Debian-based, e.g., Ubuntu):**
   - Open the terminal and run the following command:

   ```bash

   sudo apt update
   sudo apt install python3
   ```

2. **Using a Package Manager (Red Hat-based, e.g., Fedora):**
   - Run the following command in the terminal:

   ```bash

   sudo dnf install python3
   ```

3. **Verify Installation:**
   - Type `python3 --version` to verify that Python is correctly installed.

---

*Step 2: Setting Up Virtual Environments for Cross-Platform Development*

When developing cross-platform applications, it's essential to manage dependencies separately for each project. Python's virtual environments provide an isolated environment for each project, allowing you to manage dependencies and avoid conflicts between them.

Creating and Activating a Virtual Environment

1. **Install `virtualenv` (if not already installed):**
   o On any platform, you can install the `virtualenv` package using the following command:

   ```bash
   pip install virtualenv
   ```

2. **Create a Virtual Environment:**
   o Navigate to your project directory, then create a virtual environment by running:

   ```bash
   python3 -m venv myprojectenv
   ```

   Replace `myprojectenv` with the name of your environment folder.

3. **Activate the Virtual Environment:**
   o **On Windows:**

   ```bash
   myprojectenv\Scripts\activate
   ```

   o **On macOS and Linux:**

   ```bash
   ```

```
source myprojectenv/bin/activate
```

4. **Deactivate the Virtual Environment:**
   o To deactivate the virtual environment, simply run:

   ```
   bash
   ```

   ```
   deactivate
   ```

Using virtual environments ensures that you can keep project dependencies isolated and easily manage different versions of packages across projects.

Installing Required Packages

Once the virtual environment is active, you can install packages specific to your project using `pip`. For example:

```
bash
```

```
pip install kivy    # For cross-platform mobile
apps
pip install pyqt5   # For desktop apps with a
native UI
pip install flask  # For web apps
```

You can create a `requirements.txt` file to specify all the dependencies for your project:

```
bash
```

```
pip freeze > requirements.txt
```

To install the dependencies from a `requirements.txt` file:

```bash
```

```
pip install -r requirements.txt
```

---

*Step 3: Installing Essential Tools and Frameworks for Cross-Platform Development*

Python has several tools and frameworks designed to make cross-platform development easier. Below are some essential tools and frameworks you should consider for building cross-platform applications.

1. Kivy:

Kivy is an open-source Python library for building multi-touch applications, particularly suitable for mobile and desktop platforms.

- **Installation:**

  ```bash
  ```

  ```
  pip install kivy
  ```

- **Use Case:** Kivy is ideal for building mobile applications that work on both Android and iOS, as well as desktop applications for Windows, macOS, and Linux. It allows you to create interactive applications with a touch interface, making it suitable for mobile apps.

2. BeeWare:

BeeWare is a collection of tools for building native Python applications on multiple platforms. It allows you to write a single Python codebase and deploy it on macOS, Windows, Linux, iOS, and Android.

- **Installation:**

```bash
pip install beeware
```

- **Use Case:** BeeWare is useful when you want to create truly native apps with a native user interface, while still using Python for development.

3. PyQt and PySide:

These libraries provide bindings to the Qt application framework, which is known for its powerful and flexible cross-platform GUI capabilities. PyQt and PySide are used for creating desktop applications with Python that work across all major operating systems.

- **Installation:**

```bash
pip install pyqt5   # PyQt
pip install pyside2  # PySide
```

- **Use Case:** PyQt and PySide are best suited for creating cross-platform desktop applications with

54

rich graphical interfaces. They allow developers to create applications that have a native look and feel across Windows, macOS, and Linux.

### 4. Flask/Django for Web Development:

Both Flask and Django are popular Python frameworks for web development. Flask is lightweight and flexible, while Django is more feature-rich and comes with built-in tools for larger-scale applications.

- **Installation:**

  bash

  ```bash
  pip install flask   # Flask for lightweight web apps
  pip install django   # Django for larger-scale web apps
  ```

- **Use Case:** Flask and Django are essential when building cross-platform web applications. Flask is great for simple and scalable web applications, while Django is ideal for large-scale, data-driven applications.

### 5. PyInstaller and cx_Freeze for Packaging:

If you need to distribute your Python application as a standalone executable, you can use tools like PyInstaller and cx_Freeze to bundle your application into an executable file for Windows, macOS, or Linux.

- **Installation:**

```bash
bash

pip install pyinstaller
pip install cx_Freeze
```

- **Use Case:** These tools are especially useful when you want to distribute your Python application to users who might not have Python installed on their systems. They allow you to package your application into an easily distributable format for different platforms.

---

*Step 4: Managing Dependencies and Version Control*

To ensure that your Python environment is reproducible and that your codebase is well-maintained, it's essential to manage dependencies and use version control.

1. Dependency Management:

As mentioned earlier, you can use `pip` and `requirements.txt` for managing project dependencies. This ensures that anyone working on the project, or any deployment environments, have the same libraries installed.

2. Version Control with Git:

Using Git is essential for version control and collaboration on cross-platform projects.

- **Initialize Git Repository:**

```bash
git init
```

- **Commit Changes:**

```bash
git add .
git commit -m "Initial commit"
```

- **Push to Remote Repository (e.g., GitHub):**

```bash
git remote add origin <repository_url>
git push -u origin master
```

---

*Conclusion*

Setting up a Python development environment for cross-platform development involves installing Python, setting up virtual environments, and configuring essential tools and frameworks. By following these steps, you'll have a development environment that's ready to handle projects that target multiple platforms, including mobile, desktop, and web. With Python's wide array of libraries and frameworks like Kivy, BeeWare, PyQt, Flask, and Django, developers can create powerful cross-platform applications while maintaining productivity and code simplicity.

# CHAPTER 7

# SETTING UP C# DEVELOPMENT WITH VISUAL STUDIO

Visual Studio is one of the most powerful and popular Integrated Development Environments (IDEs) for C# development. It supports a wide variety of platforms, including Windows, macOS, and Linux, making it an excellent choice for cross-platform C# development. In this chapter, we'll guide you through the process of installing and configuring Visual Studio for C# development on different platforms. This setup will enable you to develop cross-platform applications using C# with tools like .NET Core, Xamarin, and .NET MAUI.

---

*Step 1: Installing Visual Studio on Different Platforms*

Installing Visual Studio on Windows

1. **Download the Installer:**
   o Visit the official Visual Studio website.
   o Click on **Download Visual Studio** and select **Visual Studio Community** (the free version) or any other version that suits your needs (Professional or Enterprise).
2. **Run the Installer:**

o After downloading, launch the installer. You will see a setup wizard that will guide you through the installation.

3. **Choose Workloads:**
   o During installation, you'll be asked to select the workloads you want to install. For C# development, the following workloads are essential:
   - **.NET Desktop Development:** For building Windows desktop applications (WPF, Windows Forms).
   - **ASP.NET and Web Development:** For building cross-platform web applications using ASP.NET Core.
   - **Mobile Development with .NET:** For cross-platform mobile development with Xamarin.
   - **Game Development with Unity:** For C# game development (if needed).

4. **Complete the Installation:**
   o After selecting the necessary workloads, click **Install**. The installer will download and configure the required components.

5. **Launch Visual Studio:**
   o Once the installation is complete, launch Visual Studio, and you're ready to start developing with C#.

Installing Visual Studio on macOS

1. **Download the Installer:**
   o Visit the Visual Studio for Mac download page.
   o Click on the **Download Visual Studio for Mac** button.

2. **Run the Installer:**
   - Open the downloaded .dmg file and drag Visual Studio into the Applications folder.
3. **Start the Installation:**
   - Launch Visual Studio from the Applications folder. You will be prompted to install additional components such as .NET SDKs and mobile development tools.
4. **Choose Workloads:**
   - For C# development, ensure you select the following workloads:
     - **.NET Core and ASP.NET Core:** For web development with C# and .NET Core.
     - **Mobile Development with .NET (Xamarin):** For cross-platform mobile development.
5. **Complete the Setup:**
   - After the installation of the necessary tools, Visual Studio for Mac will be ready for use.
6. **Launch Visual Studio for Mac:**
   - Open Visual Studio, and you're now equipped to develop cross-platform C# applications.

Installing Visual Studio on Linux

1. **Install via Snap (Ubuntu/Debian-based distros):**
   - Visual Studio for Linux is available as a preview, and you can install it through the Snap package manager.
   - Open the terminal and run:

   ```bash
   bash
   ```

```
sudo snap install --classic code
```

2. **Install via Package Manager (for Red Hat/Fedora-based distros):**
   o You can also install Visual Studio Code (a lightweight version of Visual Studio) for Linux using the following commands:

   ```bash
   ```

   ```
   sudo          rpm          --import
   https://packages.microsoft.com/keys
   /microsoft.asc
   sudo     sh     -c     'echo     -e
   "[code]\nname=Visual        Studio
   Code\nbaseurl=https://packages.micr
   osoft.com/yumrepos/vscode\nenabled=
   1\ngpgcheck=1\ngpgkey=https://packa
   ges.microsoft.com/keys/microsoft.as
   c" > /etc/yum.repos.d/vscode.repo'
   sudo dnf check-update
   sudo dnf install code
   ```

3. **Install C# Extension (Optional for Visual Studio Code):**
   o If you're using **Visual Studio Code** (the lightweight, open-source version), you'll need to install the **C# extension** for Visual Studio Code:
     ▪ Open Visual Studio Code and navigate to the Extensions view by clicking on the Extensions icon in the Activity Bar.
     ▪ Search for "C#" and install the **C# for Visual Studio Code (powered by OmniSharp)** extension.
4. **Launch Visual Studio/Visual Studio Code:**

61

o Open Visual Studio or Visual Studio Code, and you're ready to start writing cross-platform C# applications.

---

*Step 2: Configuring the Development Environment for C# Cross-Platform Development*

Once you've installed Visual Studio, you need to configure it for cross-platform development. Visual Studio offers excellent support for .NET Core, Xamarin, and .NET MAUI, which are essential for building applications across multiple platforms.

Setting Up .NET Core for Cross-Platform Development

.NET Core is a cross-platform framework for building modern, scalable applications. It can run on Windows, macOS, and Linux, and is perfect for developing web APIs, microservices, and command-line applications.

1. **Install .NET Core SDK:**
   o In Visual Studio, the .NET Core SDK is often installed automatically when you select the ".NET Core and ASP.NET Core" workload.
   o If needed, you can download the .NET Core SDK separately from the official .NET website.
2. **Create a .NET Core Project:**
   o To start a new .NET Core project in Visual Studio, go to **File → New → Project**.
   o Select **ASP.NET Core Web Application** or **Console Application** (depending on your use case).

o Follow the prompts to configure the project, ensuring that you select **.NET Core** as the framework.

## 3. Develop and Test Cross-Platform Applications:

o Visual Studio allows you to develop .NET Core applications that run on Windows, macOS, and Linux.

o Use the **Terminal** within Visual Studio (or an external terminal) to run and test the application in different operating systems.

Setting Up Xamarin for Mobile Development

Xamarin enables you to build mobile applications for Android and iOS using a single C# codebase. Visual Studio provides full support for Xamarin, including mobile device simulators, device emulators, and debugging tools.

## 1. Install Xamarin:

o When setting up Visual Studio, ensure that you install the **Mobile Development with .NET** workload. This will include Xamarin and all the necessary tools.

## 2. Create a Xamarin Project:

o In Visual Studio, go to **File → New → Project**.

o Select **Mobile App (Xamarin.Forms)** for a cross-platform mobile application or **Xamarin.Android / Xamarin.iOS** for platform-specific mobile apps.

## 3. Test and Debug:

o Visual Studio includes device emulators for testing Android and iOS apps. You can launch these emulators directly from within Visual Studio.

o   Debugging tools allow you to set breakpoints, inspect variables, and use device-specific features for both Android and iOS apps.

## Setting Up .NET MAUI for Cross-Platform UI Development

.NET MAUI (Multi-platform App UI) is the next-generation framework for building cross-platform desktop and mobile applications with a single codebase.

1.  **Install .NET MAUI:**
    o   Ensure that you select the **.NET MAUI** workload during Visual Studio installation. This includes templates and tools for developing multi-platform apps targeting Android, iOS, macOS, and Windows.
2.  **Create a .NET MAUI Project:**
    o   Open Visual Studio, go to **File → New → Project**.
    o   Select **.NET MAUI App** as the project template.
    o   You can start building your app targeting multiple platforms, with shared code for business logic and platform-specific UI components.
3.  **Run on Multiple Platforms:**
    o   Use the **Device Simulator** in Visual Studio to test your .NET MAUI application across Android, iOS, macOS, and Windows.
    o   Visual Studio allows you to run and debug the application simultaneously on different platforms, providing a seamless cross-platform development experience.

*Step 3: Using Visual Studio for C# Cross-Platform Development*

With Visual Studio set up, you can now begin developing your C# cross-platform applications. Here are a few tips and best practices to make the most of your development environment:

- **Code Completion and IntelliSense:** Visual Studio provides powerful IntelliSense features that suggest methods, properties, and even whole code snippets as you type. This makes cross-platform development easier by reducing errors and speeding up the coding process.
- **NuGet Package Manager:** Visual Studio integrates with the **NuGet Package Manager**, which allows you to easily add libraries and dependencies to your projects. You can install packages like **Xamarin**, **Entity Framework Core**, or **ASP.NET Core** to extend your application's capabilities.
- **Cross-Platform Testing:** Visual Studio provides emulators and device simulators for mobile apps (Xamarin), and the ability to test .NET Core applications on different platforms (Windows, Linux, macOS) directly within the IDE.
- **Version Control with Git:** Visual Studio has built-in Git integration, making it easy to collaborate on projects with teams. You can commit changes, branch, and merge directly from within the IDE.

*Conclusion*

Setting up Visual Studio for C# development on multiple platforms is straightforward and provides a unified environment for building cross-platform applications. Whether you're developing a web app with .NET Core, a mobile app with Xamarin, or a desktop/mobile app with .NET MAUI, Visual Studio offers the tools and support you need. By following these installation and configuration steps, you'll be ready to develop powerful, cross-platform solutions using C#.

# CHAPTER 8

# CROSS-PLATFORM IDES AND TOOLS

When developing cross-platform applications using languages like Python and C#, selecting the right Integrated Development Environment (IDE) and supporting tools can significantly improve your productivity and streamline the development process. In this chapter, we'll review some of the best IDEs and tools available for both Python and C# that support multiple platforms. These tools allow developers to write, test, debug, and deploy applications across a wide range of operating systems, including Windows, macOS, and Linux.

---

*1. Visual Studio Code (VS Code)*

**Platform Support:** Windows, macOS, Linux

**Overview:**
Visual Studio Code (VS Code) is a lightweight, open-source code editor developed by Microsoft. It is highly customizable and supports a wide variety of programming languages, including Python and C#. VS Code is an excellent choice for cross-platform development due to its flexibility, extensibility, and wide range of extensions available for both Python and C# development.

## Key Features:

- **Extensions:** VS Code supports a plethora of extensions, such as the **Python extension** for Python development and the **C# extension** (powered by OmniSharp) for C# development. These extensions provide IntelliSense, debugging capabilities, code navigation, linting, and more.
- **Integrated Terminal:** VS Code includes an integrated terminal, making it easy to run commands, test applications, and execute Python or C# scripts without leaving the IDE.
- **Version Control Integration:** VS Code has built-in Git integration, allowing you to manage repositories, commit code, and perform Git operations directly from the IDE.
- **Lightweight and Fast:** VS Code is known for being fast and resource-efficient, making it suitable for large projects and machines with limited resources.

## Use Cases:

- **Python Development:** Ideal for web development, data science, scripting, and automation with Python.
- **C# Development:** Great for .NET Core, Xamarin, and ASP.NET development.

## Installation:

- Visit the Visual Studio Code website and download the appropriate version for your platform (Windows, macOS, Linux).
- Install extensions for Python and C# by searching for them in the Extensions marketplace inside VS Code.

*2. JetBrains Rider*

**Platform Support:** Windows, macOS, Linux

**Overview:**
JetBrains Rider is a powerful, cross-platform IDE specifically designed for .NET development, including C#. It combines the features of IntelliJ IDEA and ReSharper, making it a powerful tool for C# developers working on cross-platform .NET Core, Xamarin, or Unity projects.

**Key Features:**

- **Cross-Platform .NET Development:** Rider fully supports .NET Core, ASP.NET Core, Xamarin, and Unity, making it a solid choice for cross-platform C# development.
- **Code Analysis and Refactoring:** Rider includes powerful code analysis, refactoring tools, and code completion features powered by ReSharper, making C# development easier and more efficient.
- **Integrated Debugger:** Rider includes a full-featured debugger for both .NET applications and remote debugging for cross-platform development.
- **Unit Testing Support:** Rider supports unit testing frameworks like NUnit, MSTest, and xUnit, which is crucial for ensuring code quality across multiple platforms.
- **Version Control Integration:** Rider integrates with Git, Mercurial, and other version control systems, making it easier to manage your code across multiple platforms.

## Use Cases:

- **C# Development:** Ideal for enterprise-level applications, Unity game development, Xamarin mobile applications, and .NET Core cross-platform apps.
- **Python Development (via Plugins):** While Rider is primarily focused on C#, it also supports Python development with the installation of additional plugins, making it a versatile tool for those who need to work with both languages.

## Installation:

- Visit the JetBrains Rider website to download the appropriate version for your operating system.
- Rider is a commercial product, but a free trial is available for evaluation.

---

*3. PyCharm*

**Platform Support:** Windows, macOS, Linux

**Overview:**
PyCharm is a full-featured IDE developed by JetBrains, specifically designed for Python development. It offers a wide array of tools for professional Python development, including an integrated debugger, test runner, and Git integration, among others. While it is primarily aimed at Python, PyCharm also supports C# development with the help of plugins.

**Key Features:**

- **Python-Specific Tools:** PyCharm comes with everything needed for Python development, including intelligent code completion, a powerful debugger, code navigation, and profiling tools.
- **Cross-Platform Support:** PyCharm is available on Windows, macOS, and Linux, making it suitable for teams working in different environments.
- **Integrated Virtual Environment Support:** PyCharm helps developers create and manage Python virtual environments, ensuring that dependencies and packages are isolated and portable.
- **Integrated Testing:** PyCharm supports multiple testing frameworks, including pytest, unittest, and nose.
- **Version Control Integration:** PyCharm integrates with Git, Mercurial, and other version control systems, allowing seamless version control across platforms.

## Use Cases:

- **Python Development:** PyCharm is one of the best IDEs for Python web development (using Django, Flask), data science, machine learning, and automation scripting.
- **C# Development (via Plugins):** Though not its primary focus, C# development is supported via plugins such as the **.NET Core plugin** and others that can be installed within the IDE.

## Installation:

- Visit the PyCharm website to download the community edition (free) or professional edition (paid) for your platform.

71

*4. Eclipse*

**Platform Support:** Windows, macOS, Linux

**Overview:**
Eclipse is a widely used open-source IDE that supports many programming languages, including Java, Python, C++, and C#. With the right plugins, Eclipse can be a great option for both Python and C# development, especially when developing Java-based, cross-platform, or enterprise applications.

**Key Features:**

- **Extensibility:** Eclipse's modular nature allows you to install plugins for additional languages and tools, including Python and C#. The **PyDev plugin** supports Python, and the **Eclim plugin** supports C#.
- **Cross-Platform Support:** Eclipse runs on all major platforms (Windows, macOS, Linux) and provides a consistent development environment across operating systems.
- **Integrated Version Control:** Eclipse supports Git, SVN, and other version control systems out of the box, making it easy to manage your code across platforms.
- **Project Management:** Eclipse supports robust project management tools, which is ideal for larger, enterprise-level projects.

**Use Cases:**

- **Python Development:** Eclipse with PyDev is an excellent choice for Python development, especially when dealing with large-scale projects or when integration with other languages (like Java) is required.

- **C# Development:** Eclipse can be used for C# development with the appropriate plugins, though it's more commonly used for Java. However, it's still a valid choice if you need to work with both languages.

## Installation:

- Visit the Eclipse IDE website to download the installer. Once installed, you can add plugins for Python and C# as needed.

---

*5. Sublime Text*

**Platform Support:** Windows, macOS, Linux

**Overview:**

Sublime Text is a lightweight, fast, and highly customizable text editor used by many developers. While it is not a full-fledged IDE, Sublime Text supports both Python and C# development through plugins and is particularly popular for its speed and responsiveness.

**Key Features:**

- **Syntax Highlighting and Code Completion:** Sublime Text offers syntax highlighting and autocompletion for many programming languages, including Python and C#.
- **Extensibility:** Sublime Text can be extended with a variety of plugins and packages from its **Package Control**. Popular packages include **SublimeLinter** for

linting and **Python-related packages** for debugging, testing, and code navigation.

- **Cross-Platform Support:** Sublime Text runs on all major platforms and offers a consistent experience.
- **Speed:** Sublime Text is known for being lightweight and fast, making it an excellent choice for developers working on smaller projects or scripts.

## Use Cases:

- **Python Development:** Sublime Text is perfect for Python scripting, data science, or quick coding tasks, where full IDE features are not necessary.
- **C# Development:** Sublime Text can be used for C# development with the right plugins, but it is better suited for smaller-scale projects or when you need to quickly edit code.

## Installation:

- Visit the Sublime Text website to download the editor. Once installed, you can install additional plugins through **Package Control** to extend its functionality for Python and C#.

---

*Conclusion*

Selecting the right IDE or tool for cross-platform development can significantly impact your productivity. Whether you're working with Python or C#, the tools mentioned above provide excellent support for building, testing, and deploying applications across multiple platforms.

- **VS Code** is a lightweight, highly customizable choice for both Python and C# developers, perfect for projects of all sizes.
- **JetBrains Rider** is a great option for C# developers, especially those working with .NET Core, Xamarin, and Unity, while **PyCharm** remains the go-to IDE for Python developers.
- **Eclipse** and **Sublime Text** are great alternatives, with Eclipse offering extensibility and Sublime Text providing speed and simplicity for smaller projects.

No matter the language you choose, these cross-platform IDEs and tools ensure you can develop applications efficiently across Windows, macOS, and Linux, making them ideal for modern software development.

# CHAPTER 9

# CROSS-PLATFORM IDES AND TOOLS

When developing cross-platform applications in Python and C#, the choice of Integrated Development Environment (IDE) and supporting tools is crucial to streamline workflows, improve productivity, and ensure smooth development and debugging. Fortunately, there are several cross-platform IDEs and tools that support both Python and C#, enabling developers to work seamlessly across Windows, macOS, and Linux. This chapter will review some of the best IDEs and tools that cater to both Python and C# development.

---

*1. Visual Studio Code (VS Code)*

**Platform Support:** Windows, macOS, Linux

**Overview:** Visual Studio Code (VS Code) is a lightweight, open-source code editor developed by Microsoft, which has become immensely popular due to its versatility, speed, and extensive support for various programming languages. It provides excellent support for both Python and C# through extensions, making it an ideal choice for cross-platform development.

76

## Key Features:

- **Extensibility:** VS Code supports Python and C# through dedicated extensions. The **Python extension** provides features like IntelliSense, linting, debugging, and Jupyter notebook support. The **C# extension** (powered by OmniSharp) offers code completion, debugging, and integration with .NET Core.
- **Integrated Terminal:** VS Code comes with an integrated terminal, allowing you to run Python and C# scripts or commands directly without leaving the editor.
- **Git Integration:** VS Code has built-in support for Git, enabling developers to manage version control, commit changes, and handle repositories directly from within the IDE.
- **Debugging Support:** Both Python and C# debugging features are included. You can set breakpoints, watch variables, and step through the code with full debugging tools.
- **Cross-Platform Compatibility:** VS Code is available on Windows, macOS, and Linux, providing a consistent development environment across platforms.

## Use Cases:

- **Python Development:** Ideal for web development with Flask or Django, data science with Jupyter, and scripting tasks.
- **C# Development:** Perfect for .NET Core development, Xamarin mobile development, and ASP.NET applications.

## Installation:

- Download VS Code from the official website, then install the Python and C# extensions from the marketplace.

---

*2. JetBrains Rider*

**Platform Support:** Windows, macOS, Linux

**Overview:** JetBrains Rider is a powerful, cross-platform IDE designed for .NET development, including C#. It combines the best features of the IntelliJ IDEA platform and ReSharper, a popular code analysis and refactoring tool. Rider offers full support for .NET Core, ASP.NET Core, Xamarin, and Unity, making it a robust tool for cross-platform C# development.

**Key Features:**

- **Support for .NET Framework and .NET Core:** Rider fully supports .NET Core and .NET Framework, providing tools for building web applications, mobile apps, and desktop applications across platforms.
- **Xamarin Support:** Rider provides excellent support for Xamarin, making it an ideal choice for mobile application development for Android and iOS using C#.
- **Code Analysis and Refactoring:** Powered by ReSharper, Rider offers advanced code analysis, refactoring tools, and code suggestions, helping developers write cleaner and more maintainable code.
- **Integrated Debugger:** Rider includes a powerful debugger for both C# and other .NET-based languages, along with remote debugging and testing support.

- **Cross-Platform Support:** Available on Windows, macOS, and Linux, Rider ensures that developers can work seamlessly across platforms.

## Use Cases:

- **C# Development:** Ideal for enterprise-level applications, Xamarin mobile apps, Unity game development, and ASP.NET Core applications.
- **Python Development (via Plugins):** While Rider is primarily geared towards C#, Python support can be added through plugins, but it may not be as feature-rich as dedicated Python IDEs.

## Installation:

- Visit the JetBrains Rider website to download and install. Rider offers a free trial, with paid versions available after the trial period.

---

*3. PyCharm*

**Platform Support:** Windows, macOS, Linux

**Overview:** PyCharm, developed by JetBrains, is one of the most popular IDEs for Python development. It provides a full range of tools to support Python developers in web development, data science, and other Python-related tasks. Although PyCharm is mainly designed for Python, it can also be configured to work with C# using the appropriate plugins.

## Key Features:

- **Python-Specific Features:** PyCharm offers intelligent code completion, powerful debugging, testing frameworks, and a built-in terminal. It is ideal for developing Python applications with frameworks like Django and Flask.
- **Cross-Platform Support:** Available on Windows, macOS, and Linux, PyCharm enables a consistent development environment for Python development on all platforms.
- **Integrated Virtual Environment Management:** PyCharm makes it easy to manage Python virtual environments and dependencies, ensuring that each project has its isolated setup.
- **Unit Testing and Debugging:** Supports various testing frameworks like pytest and unittest and integrates with Python's built-in debugging tools.
- **Plugin Support for C#:** PyCharm does not natively support C#, but C# development can be set up using external plugins like **ReSharper** or **.NET Core plugin**, although these plugins are more commonly associated with other JetBrains products like Rider.

## Use Cases:

- **Python Development:** Perfect for web development, data science, machine learning, and automation projects.
- **C# Development (via Plugins):** PyCharm can support basic C# development, but its feature set for C# will be limited compared to specialized C# IDEs.

## Installation:

- Download PyCharm from <u>the official website</u>, then install the necessary plugins for C# development if needed.

---

*4. Eclipse IDE*

**Platform Support:** Windows, macOS, Linux

**Overview:** Eclipse is a popular, open-source IDE primarily known for Java development. However, it supports a wide range of programming languages through plugins, including Python and C#. With the right configuration, Eclipse can be used for both Python and C# development, making it a versatile tool for cross-platform development.

**Key Features:**

- **Extensibility:** Eclipse is highly extensible, with support for a wide variety of programming languages and development tools through plugins. The **PyDev plugin** adds Python support, and **Eclim** adds support for C# development.
- **Cross-Platform Support:** Eclipse works on Windows, macOS, and Linux, providing a consistent development environment across platforms.
- **Integrated Version Control:** Eclipse includes built-in support for Git, SVN, and other version control systems, making it easy to manage projects across multiple platforms.
- **Powerful Refactoring and Debugging:** Eclipse offers robust refactoring tools, a powerful debugger, and code analysis features for both Python and C# development.

81

## Use Cases:

- **Python Development:** Eclipse with the PyDev plugin is great for Python development, especially when working with larger codebases or when Java integration is needed.
- **C# Development:** Eclipse with Eclim or other plugins can be used for basic C# development, but it's not as optimized as Rider or Visual Studio for C#.

## Installation:

- Download Eclipse from the official website, and install the necessary plugins (PyDev for Python, Eclim for C#) to extend functionality.

---

*5. Sublime Text*

**Platform Support:** Windows, macOS, Linux

**Overview:** Sublime Text is a lightweight, fast, and highly customizable text editor used by developers around the world. While it is not a full-fledged IDE, it supports both Python and C# development through plugins. It's particularly favored for its speed and ease of use, making it a great choice for developers working on smaller projects or needing a quick code editor.

## Key Features:

- **Syntax Highlighting:** Sublime Text offers syntax highlighting and autocompletion for Python and C# right out of the box.

- **Cross-Platform Support:** Sublime Text works on Windows, macOS, and Linux, ensuring that developers can use it regardless of their operating system.
- **Extensibility:** Sublime Text can be extended with a wide variety of plugins via **Package Control**, including Python and C# tools such as **SublimeLinter** (for linting) and **OmniSharp** (for C# development).
- **Speed:** Sublime Text is known for its lightweight nature and fast performance, making it an excellent choice for quick edits and smaller projects.

**Use Cases:**

- **Python Development:** Great for quick Python scripting, data analysis, or editing small Python projects.
- **C# Development:** Can be used for C# development with the help of plugins, but it is not as fully featured as other IDEs for large-scale C# projects.

**Installation:**

- Download Sublime Text from the official website, and install plugins through **Package Control** for Python and C# support.

---

*Conclusion*

Selecting the right IDE or tool for cross-platform development is crucial to ensure an efficient and productive workflow. Here's a summary of the best IDEs and tools that support both Python and C# across various platforms:

- **Visual Studio Code**: Lightweight, extensible, and excellent for both Python and C# development with the right extensions.
- **JetBrains Rider**: Powerful and feature-rich, perfect for C# developers, especially those working with Xamarin, Unity, and .NET Core. Also supports Python with plugins.
- **PyCharm**: Best for Python development, with some support for C# through plugins.
- **Eclipse**: Highly extensible, suitable for developers needing a robust tool that supports both Python and C# through plugins.
- **Sublime Text**: A fast and lightweight editor, ideal for small projects and quick edits in both Python and C#.

These tools provide the flexibility and power to develop cross-platform applications, enabling developers to efficiently work with Python and C# across Windows, macOS, and Linux.

# CHAPTER 10

# VERSION CONTROL AND COLLABORATION IN CROSS-PLATFORM PROJECTS

In modern software development, version control is a critical practice, especially for cross-platform projects that require collaboration among developers working on different operating systems and platforms. Version control systems (VCS) help developers manage changes to the codebase, track history, collaborate effectively, and ensure the integrity of the software. Git, the most widely used version control system, is particularly powerful for managing cross-platform projects, offering a distributed workflow, support for branches, and integration with services like GitHub and GitLab.

This chapter covers the best practices for using Git and other version control systems in a cross-platform context, ensuring smooth collaboration and efficient code management.

*1. Why Version Control Is Essential for Cross-Platform Projects*

For cross-platform development, version control helps in the following ways:

- **Collaboration:** Multiple developers, often working on different platforms (Windows, macOS, Linux), can contribute to the same project without conflicting changes.
- **Consistency Across Platforms:** Git allows you to keep your codebase consistent across platforms, ensuring that features and fixes are applied uniformly, regardless of the developer's operating system.
- **Branching and Merging:** Git's powerful branching and merging system allow developers to work on different tasks or features in parallel without disrupting the main codebase.
- **Backup and Recovery:** Git tracks every change, making it easy to revert to previous versions of the code in case of errors or bugs, which is vital when working on multiple platforms.
- **Automating Deployment:** Integrating version control with Continuous Integration/Continuous Deployment (CI/CD) pipelines helps streamline deployments across different platforms.

*2. Best Practices for Using Git in Cross-Platform Projects*

a. Consistent Workflow Across Platforms

- **Choose a Unified Git Workflow:** Whether you're working with GitHub, GitLab, or Bitbucket, ensure that all team members are using a consistent workflow. The most commonly used workflows for cross-platform projects are:
  - **Feature Branch Workflow:** Each new feature or bug fix is developed in a separate branch. Once

the task is complete, the branch is merged into the main branch (usually `master` or `main`).

- o **Git Flow Workflow:** A more structured workflow that uses several long-lived branches like `develop`, `feature`, `release`, and `hotfix` for a more organized approach to collaboration and versioning.
- o **Forking Workflow:** Common for open-source projects where contributors fork the main repository, work on their changes, and submit pull requests.

- **Adopt a Code Review Process:** Use pull requests (PRs) or merge requests (MRs) to review code before merging it into the main codebase. This ensures that changes are peer-reviewed and validated, which is especially important when developers are working from different platforms.

b. Managing Line Endings Across Platforms

- **Handle Line Endings Consistently:** Different operating systems use different characters for line endings. Windows uses CRLF (carriage return + line feed), while macOS and Linux use LF (line feed). Inconsistent line endings can lead to issues when merging code from developers using different platforms.
    - o **Use `.gitattributes` File:** To avoid problems with line endings, configure Git to handle line endings consistently across platforms. You can do this by adding a `.gitattributes` file to the root of your repository and specifying the following settings:

87

```bash
* text=auto
*.c text
*.cpp text
*.py text
*.cs text
*.html text
*.css text
*.js text
```

This configuration ensures that all text files use LF line endings, regardless of the platform the code is committed from.

- **Ensure Consistent Development Environment:** Using Docker or a virtualized development environment can ensure that all developers are working in similar conditions, regardless of their underlying OS.

c. Use Descriptive Commit Messages

- **Write Clear, Concise Commit Messages:** Good commit messages are essential for tracking changes and ensuring clarity when reviewing the project history. A commit message should explain *why* the change was made, not just *what* was changed.
  - **Follow a Standard Convention:** For example, use the following structure:
    - **Type:** Indicates the type of change (e.g., feat, fix, docs, chore).
    - **Scope:** (Optional) Describes the part of the project being modified (e.g., api, UI).

▪ **Message:** A brief description of the change.

Example:

```bash
bash
```

```
feat(ui):   add   login   button   to
homepage
fix(api):   resolve   bug   with   user
authentication
docs(readme):   update   installation
instructions
```

d. Use `.gitignore` to Exclude Platform-Specific Files

- **Exclude Files Specific to Each Platform:** Each operating system may generate different temporary files, caches, or configurations. For example, macOS creates `.DS_Store` files, while Windows uses `Thumbs.db`. These files should not be included in the codebase.

  o **Configure `.gitignore` Properly:** Add a `.gitignore` file to the root of your repository to exclude these unnecessary files. GitHub offers templates for `.gitignore` files specific to different programming languages and operating systems.

    Example `.gitignore` for a Python and C# project:

```python
python
```

```
# Python
*.pyc
__pycache__/
```

89

```
# C#
bin/
obj/

# macOS
.DS_Store

# Windows
Thumbs.db
```

e. Resolve Merge Conflicts Quickly

- **Avoid Conflicts with Frequent Pulls:** Regularly pull changes from the remote repository to keep your local up to date. This helps avoid conflicts, especially when multiple developers are working on the same file or section of code.
- **Use Merge Tools:** When conflicts occur, use merge tools such as **KDiff3**, **Meld**, or **Visual Studio Code's built-in merge tool** to manually resolve conflicts. This ensures that the changes from both developers are preserved appropriately.

---

*3. Collaborative Tools for Cross-Platform Projects*

a. GitHub, GitLab, and Bitbucket

- **GitHub:** The most popular Git hosting service, GitHub offers powerful collaboration features, including issue tracking, pull requests, code reviews, and CI/CD integrations.
- **GitLab:** GitLab provides a comprehensive set of tools for Git repositories, including integrated CI/CD pipelines, issue tracking, and an extensive set of DevOps tools.

- **Bitbucket:** Another popular Git hosting service, Bitbucket integrates well with other Atlassian tools like Jira, making it an excellent choice for teams already using Atlassian products.

## b. Continuous Integration/Continuous Deployment (CI/CD)

- **Jenkins, Travis CI, CircleCI:** These CI/CD tools automate the testing, building, and deployment processes, ensuring that your code is continuously integrated and delivered across platforms.
- **GitHub Actions:** GitHub Actions allows you to automate workflows directly within your GitHub repository, making it easy to set up CI/CD pipelines for cross-platform development.

## c. Code Review and Issue Tracking Tools

- **Pull Requests and Merge Requests:** Pull requests (GitHub) or merge requests (GitLab) are essential for code reviews. These tools allow team members to discuss changes, track feedback, and ensure that only high-quality code is merged into the main branch.
- **Jira, Trello, and Asana:** These project management tools help teams track tasks, sprints, and bug reports across platforms. They integrate seamlessly with Git repositories to connect commits, branches, and pull requests to project tickets.

*4. Handling Cross-Platform Builds with Git*

For cross-platform projects, it's crucial to set up a build process that works on different platforms. Git and CI/CD tools can help automate the process:

- **Use Platform-Agnostic Build Tools:** Tools like **CMake** (for C++/C#) and **Make** (for Unix-based systems) allow you to create platform-independent build configurations.
- **Docker for Consistent Environments:** Docker enables you to build and deploy applications in containers, ensuring consistency across all development environments. It is especially useful when different platforms (e.g., Windows and Linux) need to build the same code.

*Conclusion*

Version control is an essential tool for managing cross-platform projects. By using Git and other version control systems effectively, you ensure that your codebase remains consistent and maintainable across multiple platforms. Best practices such as consistent workflows, handling line endings, using `.gitignore`, writing clear commit messages, and leveraging CI/CD tools help improve collaboration and streamline the development process for teams working on different operating systems. With these practices in place, your cross-platform project will be easier to manage, collaborate on, and maintain.

# CHAPTER 11

# *CROSS-PLATFORM USER INTERFACE DESIGN PRINCIPLES*

Designing user interfaces (UI) for cross-platform applications presents unique challenges. Each platform (Windows, macOS, Linux, Android, iOS) has its own set of user interface conventions, visual aesthetics, and usability standards. However, cross-platform development requires that your application provides a consistent and seamless experience across all these platforms without having to redesign the interface for each one.

In this chapter, we will explore key principles for designing user interfaces that work well across multiple platforms while maintaining a native feel and providing a consistent experience for users.

---

## 1. Consistency Across Platforms

Consistency is one of the most important principles of cross-platform UI design. While each platform may have its own unique characteristics, your application should deliver a consistent user experience across all platforms. This doesn't mean the UI should be identical everywhere, but it should have a unified style, functionality, and interaction pattern.

### How to achieve consistency:

- **Consistent Layouts:** Keep layout structures similar across platforms. Use grid systems, flexible containers, and responsive design principles to adapt layouts to different screen sizes and resolutions.
- **Color and Typography:** Maintain a consistent color palette and typography. While you might adjust the font size to suit different platforms, the core visual identity should remain the same.
- **Standardized Icons:** Use icons that are universally recognized and supported across all platforms. Tools like Font Awesome or Material Icons provide scalable, cross-platform icons that look good on both mobile and desktop.
- **Interaction Patterns:** Ensure that interaction patterns (e.g., gestures, buttons, navigation) are consistent. While swiping is a common interaction on mobile, desktop platforms often use clicks or keyboard shortcuts. Designing with these differences in mind while maintaining consistency in function is key.

*2. Native Look and Feel*

Even though the goal of cross-platform development is to maintain consistency, it's essential to ensure your app feels "native" on each platform. This means respecting the platform-specific UI guidelines and elements to give users a sense of familiarity, which helps improve usability and user satisfaction.

### How to achieve a native look and feel:

94

- **Use Platform-Specific UI Components:** Frameworks like Xamarin, Flutter, or React Native allow you to use native components that match the platform's look and feel. For instance, use iOS's `UIButton` and Android's `Button` for buttons instead of a generic control.
- **Follow Platform Guidelines:**
  - **iOS (Human Interface Guidelines):** Apple's guidelines emphasize clarity, depth, and simplicity. Design elements like tab bars, navigation bars, and switches should be in line with iOS standards.
  - **Android (Material Design Guidelines):** Android follows Material Design principles, which are based on grid-based layouts, bold colors, and responsive animations.
  - **Windows (Fluent Design System):** For Windows apps, use the Fluent Design System to ensure your app fits seamlessly with Windows 10's look and feel.

By following these platform guidelines, your app will look and behave the way users expect, whether they are on mobile or desktop, helping improve usability.

---

*3. Responsive Design*

Responsive design is essential for cross-platform applications as it ensures that the app's UI adapts to various screen sizes, orientations, and resolutions. This is particularly important when dealing with both mobile devices and desktop applications.

## How to implement responsive design:

- **Fluid Layouts:** Use flexible layouts that automatically adjust to different screen sizes. For example, use percentage-based widths or CSS Grid/Flexbox for web-based applications.
- **Adaptive UI Elements:** Adapt UI elements like buttons, text boxes, and images to ensure they are readable and usable across different devices. For mobile devices, make sure buttons are large enough for touch interaction, and on desktops, allow for more detailed control with smaller UI elements.
- **Breakpoints:** Define specific breakpoints for your layout depending on the screen size. Mobile screens have smaller breakpoints, while tablets and desktops have larger ones.
- **Orientation Handling:** Consider how the app behaves in portrait and landscape orientations, especially for mobile and tablet platforms. Design your UI to reflow and rearrange appropriately.

Tools like **CSS media queries**, **Flexbox**, **Grid**, and **Media Queries in Flutter** make it easy to create layouts that adapt to various platforms and screen sizes.

---

*4. Minimize Platform-Specific Customization*

While it's essential to respect platform-specific guidelines, excessive platform customization can introduce complexity and maintenance issues. Ideally, your cross-platform app should share most of the UI components across platforms and only customize the elements when necessary.

**How to minimize customization:**

- **Use Cross-Platform UI Frameworks:** Leverage frameworks like **React Native**, **Flutter**, and **Xamarin.Forms** that allow you to create shared components for multiple platforms with minimal customization. These frameworks provide built-in UI elements that adapt to the platform.
- **Component Abstraction:** Create a common abstraction layer for UI components that can handle platform-specific styles internally. For example, you might have a `Button` component in your codebase that automatically adapts to the style of each platform (rounded corners for iOS, square buttons for Android).
- **Conditional Platform Features:** Use conditional logic to apply platform-specific customizations only where absolutely necessary, like adding platform-specific navigation or UI behaviors.

By minimizing platform-specific customizations, you reduce the risk of bugs and make your codebase more maintainable.

---

*5. Prioritize Usability and Accessibility*

When designing user interfaces, it's essential to focus on both usability and accessibility to ensure that your app is intuitive and usable by all people, including those with disabilities. Cross-platform applications should take into account the different accessibility features provided by each platform.

**How to improve usability and accessibility:**

- **Keyboard and Mouse Support:** Ensure that your application works well with both touch (mobile) and mouse/keyboard (desktop) input methods. For example, implement appropriate hover effects and keyboard navigation for desktop apps.
- **Screen Readers and Voice Assistance:** Implement accessibility features like **screen readers** (for visually impaired users) and **voice commands**. For iOS, use VoiceOver, and for Android, use TalkBack.
- **High Contrast and Color Blindness Support:** Make sure that your app supports high-contrast color schemes for users with vision impairments. You should also test your app with various color blindness simulators to ensure that color is not the sole method of conveying critical information.

Frameworks like **React Native** and **Xamarin** have built-in accessibility features that allow developers to improve accessibility across platforms.

---

*6. Performance Optimization*

Performance is crucial for cross-platform UI design. While designing for multiple platforms, it's easy to lose track of performance, especially when using a shared codebase. Slow or laggy UI can result in poor user experiences.

**How to optimize performance:**

- **Efficient Rendering:** Use efficient rendering techniques like lazy loading and deferred rendering for images and heavy UI components to reduce initial load times.
- **Minimize Re-Renders:** In frameworks like React Native, ensure that your UI components don't re-render unnecessarily, which can impact performance, especially on mobile devices.
- **Optimize Animations:** Ensure that animations are smooth and do not affect app performance. For mobile apps, avoid complex animations that could drain battery life and processing power.

Tools like **Flipper** (for React Native) and **Xamarin Profiler** can help you track performance bottlenecks and optimize UI rendering across platforms.

---

*7. Test Across Platforms*

Testing is key to ensuring that your cross-platform user interface performs consistently across different platforms. It's essential to test on multiple devices and screen sizes to ensure the UI is responsive, functional, and user-friendly.

**How to conduct cross-platform testing:**

- **Device Emulators/Simulators:** Use emulators for mobile apps (like **Xcode Simulator** or **Android Emulator**) and desktop app simulators to test on multiple screen sizes and devices.
- **Real Device Testing:** While emulators are useful, testing on real devices is crucial to catching platform-specific

issues. Ensure your team tests the app on various devices, including smartphones, tablets, and desktop computers.

- **Automated UI Testing:** Use automated testing tools to ensure that UI components work as expected across different platforms. Tools like **Appium**, **XCUITest**, and **Espresso** can be used for automated UI tests in cross-platform environments.

---

*Conclusion*

Designing user interfaces for cross-platform applications requires balancing consistency and customization. By following the principles of consistency, responsiveness, and usability, and using tools that respect platform-specific guidelines, you can create seamless, native-like user interfaces across multiple platforms. Prioritizing accessibility, minimizing platform-specific customizations, and optimizing for performance will help deliver an experience that users expect, regardless of the device or platform they are using.

Cross-platform UI design isn't about making every platform look the same; it's about making every platform feel right and providing a cohesive, intuitive experience for all users.

# CHAPTER 12

# WORKING WITH DATABASES IN CROSS-PLATFORM APPLICATIONS

One of the most important aspects of cross-platform application development is ensuring seamless data management and synchronization across different platforms (Windows, macOS, Linux, Android, iOS). Databases play a crucial role in modern applications, whether for storing user data, application settings, or transaction records. However, managing databases in cross-platform environments requires specific considerations regarding data access, consistency, and synchronization.

In this chapter, we will discuss the key considerations when working with databases in cross-platform applications, including database design, synchronization techniques, and tools for managing data access across different platforms.

---

*1. Database Types for Cross-Platform Applications*

When working with databases in cross-platform applications, the first step is choosing the right type of database. The decision depends on the nature of the application, the data storage requirements, and the level of complexity required for your project.

a. Relational Databases

Relational databases are a great choice for applications that require structured data storage and complex queries. Common relational databases like **SQLite**, **MySQL**, and **PostgreSQL** are widely supported and can be accessed from various platforms.

- **SQLite:** A popular embedded database that works on Android, iOS, macOS, Linux, and Windows. SQLite is serverless, lightweight, and uses a single file for database storage, making it a great option for mobile and desktop applications.
- **MySQL/PostgreSQL:** These are full-fledged relational databases suitable for applications with more advanced data requirements. They are best for server-based applications and provide robust querying, scalability, and data integrity features.

b. NoSQL Databases

NoSQL databases are ideal for applications that require flexible, scalable data storage, particularly when the data structure is not easily represented in a relational model. Popular NoSQL databases include **MongoDB**, **Couchbase**, and **Firebase**.

- **MongoDB:** A document-based database that stores data in JSON-like format, making it ideal for unstructured data. It supports cross-platform development and can scale horizontally to handle high volumes of data.

- **Firebase:** Firebase Realtime Database and Firestore are cloud-hosted NoSQL databases that offer synchronization across devices, making them an excellent choice for mobile applications with real-time data requirements.

## c. Cloud Databases

Cloud databases offer the flexibility of managed services, where database infrastructure, scalability, and synchronization are handled by the cloud provider. They are ideal for applications that need to store data remotely and synchronize data across devices.

- **Amazon DynamoDB, Google Cloud Firestore, and Azure Cosmos DB** offer scalable and reliable cloud-based database solutions for cross-platform applications, particularly when dealing with mobile apps, web apps, and IoT applications.

---

## 2. Data Access Considerations for Cross-Platform Development

When developing cross-platform applications, data access must be efficient and consistent across platforms. Some important considerations for data access include:

### a. Data Access Libraries and Frameworks

Many programming languages offer data access libraries that work across different platforms. For Python, **SQLAlchemy** and **Django ORM** are popular libraries for accessing relational databases, while **PyMongo** is used for MongoDB. For C#, **Entity Framework Core** is the primary Object-Relational Mapper (ORM) for accessing relational databases, and **MongoDB C# Driver** is used for MongoDB.

- **SQLAlchemy (Python):** A SQL toolkit and Object-Relational Mapper (ORM) that allows developers to interact with relational databases using Python.
- **Entity Framework Core (C#):** A popular ORM that helps developers work with databases in C#. It supports cross-platform development by working with .NET Core and is ideal for building scalable applications.

b. Platform-Specific Data Access API

While using cross-platform frameworks like **Xamarin** or **Flutter**, platform-specific APIs may need to be used to access device-specific databases or handle offline storage. For example:

- On iOS and Android, you might use SQLite for local storage or **Realm** for more advanced database functionality.
- Xamarin allows you to access SQLite databases using **SQLite.NET** or through libraries like **Akavache** for local caching.

c. Data Caching and Offline Access

For mobile and desktop applications, caching data locally is crucial for performance and offline access. You can cache data using local databases like **SQLite, Realm**, or cloud-based databases like **Firebase**.

## Offline access strategies:

- **Local Data Storage:** Store data on the device to allow the application to function without an internet connection. When the connection is available, sync the data with the remote server or database.
- **Sync Mechanisms:** Use synchronization tools or libraries like **Firebase Sync**, **Microsoft Sync Framework**, or custom-built solutions to keep data in sync between local and remote databases.

---

*3. Data Synchronization Across Platforms*

In cross-platform applications, synchronizing data between devices, servers, and databases is often required, especially for mobile apps or applications that work offline. Syncing data between different platforms (e.g., between mobile devices and a central server) introduces challenges in terms of data consistency, conflict resolution, and performance.

a. Real-Time Data Synchronization

For applications that require real-time data updates across multiple devices, cloud-based databases such as **Firebase Firestore** and **MongoDB Atlas** can automatically synchronize data in real-time.

- **Firebase Firestore:** Firestore offers a powerful real-time database service, allowing apps to automatically sync data between multiple devices, even while offline. Firestore works seamlessly with Firebase SDKs and can be easily integrated into mobile applications.

- **MongoDB Atlas:** MongoDB Atlas offers cloud databases that provide real-time synchronization of data between different platforms. You can use the **MongoDB Realm SDK** to sync data between mobile applications and MongoDB servers.

### b. Conflict Resolution and Data Integrity

One of the challenges of cross-platform data synchronization is ensuring data integrity, especially when two users edit the same data on different platforms while offline. Conflict resolution is essential to ensure the application behaves predictably.

- **Timestamp-based Resolution:** When data conflicts occur, use timestamps or versioning to determine which version of the data should be retained.
- **Merge Strategies:** Define a strategy to merge conflicting changes. For example, you can keep both versions of the data and notify the user of the conflict, or you can choose the most recent change.
- **Two-Phase Commit:** Use a two-phase commit protocol for critical operations that require atomic transactions across platforms to ensure data consistency.

### c. Offline-First Architecture

Building offline-first applications ensures that users can continue working even when the network is unavailable. Data is synchronized with the server once the device regains connectivity.

- **Offline Data Persistence:** Cache data locally on the device using local databases (e.g., SQLite, Realm) or file-based storage.
- **Sync Logic:** Implement synchronization logic that ensures data is merged and updated across devices when network connectivity is restored. This often involves background tasks that check for internet access and sync data when available.

---

*4. Managing Database Connections and Performance*

Cross-platform applications need to manage database connections efficiently to ensure optimal performance, especially when working with cloud databases or remote servers.

a. Connection Pooling

Connection pooling helps manage database connections efficiently by reusing existing connections rather than opening and closing new ones for each request. This can significantly improve the performance of your application, especially in high-traffic environments.

b. Asynchronous Database Queries

Asynchronous queries help ensure that the application remains responsive while database operations are being executed. Use asynchronous methods in frameworks like **Entity Framework Core** (C#) or **async/await** in Python with libraries like **aiomysql** for MySQL or **aiopg** for PostgreSQL.

- **C# Example (Entity Framework Core):**

```csharp
csharp

var        products        =        await
context.Products.ToListAsync();
```

- **Python Example (asyncpg for PostgreSQL):**

```python
python

import asyncio
import asyncpg

async def fetch_data():
    conn              =              await
asyncpg.connect(user='user',
password='password', database='database')
    rows = await conn.fetch('SELECT * FROM
products')
    await conn.close()
    return rows

asyncio.run(fetch_data())
```

c. Caching for Performance

To reduce the number of database queries and improve performance, use caching strategies such as in-memory caching (e.g., **Redis**) or local caching with SQLite for frequently accessed data.

- **Redis:** A widely used in-memory data store that can cache frequently accessed data, reducing the need to perform repeated queries on the database.
- **SQLite for Mobile/Local Caching:** Store data locally on the device and sync it with the server when needed.

*5. Best Practices for Database Access in Cross-Platform Applications*

- **Use ORM (Object-Relational Mapping):** Use an ORM like **Entity Framework Core** (C#) or **SQLAlchemy** (Python) to abstract away the database interactions and improve maintainability.
- **Separation of Concerns:** Keep the database access layer separate from the application logic to improve modularity and make it easier to change or replace databases without affecting the core functionality.
- **Data Encryption:** Always encrypt sensitive data, both at rest and in transit, to protect user information. Use encryption libraries like **AES** or **SSL/TLS** for secure communication between the client and server.
- **Versioning Database Schemas:** Use database migration tools (e.g., **Flyway**, **Entity Framework Migrations**) to manage schema changes and ensure compatibility across different versions of the database.

*Conclusion*

Working with databases in cross-platform applications involves several considerations, including choosing the right database type, managing data access across platforms, and ensuring synchronization between local and remote data. By leveraging the appropriate tools, frameworks, and strategies, you can efficiently manage databases in cross-platform apps while ensuring optimal performance, data consistency, and a seamless user experience. Whether you choose a relational database like SQLite, a NoSQL database like Firebase, or a cloud-based solution like MongoDB Atlas, understanding and implementing the best practices for database management will help you build reliable and scalable cross-platform applications.

# CHAPTER 13

# ERROR HANDLING AND DEBUGGING ACROSS PLATFORMS

Error handling and debugging are crucial components of software development, especially in cross-platform applications where developers work across various platforms (Windows, macOS, Linux, Android, iOS). Identifying, handling, and resolving errors effectively ensures a smoother development experience, higher-quality software, and a better user experience.

In this chapter, we'll cover the best practices for error handling and debugging for both Python and C# applications in cross-platform environments, addressing platform-specific challenges and universal strategies.

---

*1. Error Handling Best Practices*

Proper error handling allows applications to gracefully handle unexpected issues without crashing and provides users with useful feedback. It's essential to have a consistent and well-designed error handling strategy, especially in cross-platform applications, where platform differences may affect how errors are raised, logged, or handled.

a. Python Error Handling Best Practices

In Python, errors are represented by exceptions. The primary mechanism for catching exceptions is the `try...except` block. Below are some best practices for error handling in Python:

- **Use Specific Exceptions:** Always catch specific exceptions rather than using a generic `except Exception` block. This makes your error handling more precise and prevents masking other errors.

```python
try:
    result = 10 / 0
except ZeroDivisionError as e:
    print(f"Error: {e}")
```

- **Log Errors Appropriately:** Logging is essential for diagnosing issues, especially in production environments. Use Python's built-in `logging` module to log exceptions and errors with appropriate severity levels (DEBUG, INFO, WARNING, ERROR, CRITICAL).

```python
import logging

logging.basicConfig(level=logging.ERROR)

try:
    10 / 0
except ZeroDivisionError as e:
```

112

```
logging.error(f"Error occurred: {e}")
```

- **Handle Platform-Specific Errors:** When developing cross-platform applications, platform-specific exceptions (such as file system errors or OS-specific issues) can arise. Handle these appropriately by checking the platform and managing errors based on the system environment.

```python
import os

if os.name == 'nt':   # For Windows
    try:
        with open('file.txt', 'r') as f:
            data = f.read()
    except OSError as e:
        print(f"Error reading file: {e}")
```

- **Graceful Failure and User Feedback:** For user-facing applications, ensure that critical errors provide meaningful feedback to the user without crashing the application. For example, use `try...except` blocks to catch errors and display a user-friendly message.

b. C# Error Handling Best Practices

In C#, error handling is done through **exceptions** and can be managed using `try...catch` blocks. Here are some best practices for error handling in C#:

- **Catch Specific Exceptions:** Just like in Python, avoid catching all exceptions with `catch`

113

`(Exception ex)`. Instead, catch specific exceptions based on the error type to handle them accordingly.

csharp

```csharp
try
{
    int result = 10 / 0;
}
catch (DivideByZeroException ex)
{
    Console.WriteLine($"Error:
{ex.Message}");
}
```

- Use **`finally`** **for Cleanup:** The `finally` block in C# ensures that resources like file handles, database connections, or network streams are closed or released regardless of whether an exception occurs.

csharp

```csharp
FileStream file = null;
try
{
    file   =   new   FileStream("file.txt",
FileMode.Open);
}
catch (IOException ex)
{
    Console.WriteLine($"IO          Error:
{ex.Message}");
}
finally
{
    file?.Close();
}
```

- **Log Errors Using a Logging Framework:** C# provides logging libraries like **NLog** and **Serilog**, which can be used to log errors and provide valuable insights for debugging. You can configure logging to write error details to a file, database, or even remote servers.

csharp

```
var logger = LogManager.GetCurrentClassLogger();

try
{
    int result = 10 / 0;
}
catch (DivideByZeroException ex)
{
    logger.Error(ex, "An error occurred while dividing.");
}
```

- **Platform-Specific Error Handling:** For cross-platform C# apps (e.g., using Xamarin or .NET MAUI), handle platform-specific errors by checking the operating system or environment and dealing with OS-specific errors (e.g., permissions issues, file access) accordingly.

csharp

```
if (Device.RuntimePlatform == Device.iOS)
{
    try
    {
```

```
        File.ReadAllText("file.txt");
    }
    catch (IOException ex)
    {
        Console.WriteLine($"iOS-specific
error: {ex.Message}");
    }
}
```

---

*2. Debugging Best Practices*

Debugging across different platforms can be challenging due to platform-specific behaviors, but there are tools and techniques that can help streamline the process and ensure a smooth debugging experience.

a. Python Debugging Best Practices

Python provides powerful debugging tools that can be used to diagnose issues in cross-platform applications:

- **Using `pdb` (Python Debugger):** The built-in `pdb` module allows you to step through your code and inspect variables interactively. To use it, insert `import pdb; pdb.set_trace()` where you want to start the debugging session.

  ```python
  import pdb

  def divide(a, b):
      pdb.set_trace()
      return a / b
  ```

116

```
divide(10, 0)
```

- **Use `logging` for Traceability:** For cross-platform apps, add logs at key points in your code to trace execution. Logging provides visibility into how your application is behaving and can help isolate issues across different platforms.
- **IDE Debugging:** Modern Python IDEs like **PyCharm**, **VS Code**, and **Eclipse** provide built-in debugging tools that allow for visual stepping through the code, variable inspection, and breakpoint management.
- **Cross-Platform Debugging:** When debugging across platforms, ensure that your application is run in different environments (e.g., on both Linux and macOS for a Python desktop app) to identify platform-specific issues.

b. C# Debugging Best Practices

C# offers several debugging tools and techniques that are essential for troubleshooting cross-platform applications:

- **Visual Studio Debugger:** Visual Studio provides one of the most powerful debuggers for C#. It supports breakpoints, watch windows, variable inspection, call stacks, and remote debugging for Xamarin and .NET Core applications.
  - o **Breakpoints:** Set breakpoints in your code and step through your application, inspecting variables and control flow.

117

- o **Conditional Breakpoints:** Use conditional breakpoints to stop execution only when certain conditions are met (e.g., when a specific variable has a particular value).
- **Remote Debugging (Xamarin/Android/iOS):** For cross-platform apps built with Xamarin, Visual Studio allows remote debugging for Android and iOS devices, making it easy to troubleshoot issues that only occur on physical devices or mobile platforms.
  - o **Xamarin Debugger:** Use Xamarin's built-in debugger to run and debug Android and iOS apps directly from Visual Studio. This debugger allows you to inspect objects, set breakpoints, and step through mobile code.
- **Logging for Cross-Platform Debugging:** Like in Python, logging is critical for debugging cross-platform C# applications. Use libraries like **Serilog** or **NLog** to log application behavior and errors in different environments (e.g., Android, iOS, Windows).

---

*3. Tools for Cross-Platform Debugging and Error Reporting*

When developing cross-platform applications, it's useful to have tools that can help you debug and handle errors across various platforms consistently:

a. Cross-Platform Error Reporting Tools

- **Sentry:** Sentry is a popular error monitoring tool that supports both Python and C#. It provides real-time error tracking and diagnostics, offering deep insights into exceptions, performance issues, and crash reports across platforms (web, mobile, desktop).
- **Raygun:** Raygun is another excellent tool for error tracking and reporting. It integrates with multiple platforms, including Python and C#, and provides detailed stack traces, user session data, and crash reporting across different devices and environments.

b. Remote Debugging and Log Aggregation Tools

- **Loggly, ELK Stack (Elasticsearch, Logstash, Kibana):** These tools help aggregate logs from different platforms and allow for powerful querying and visualization. Log aggregation helps identify patterns and issues that span multiple platforms.
- **Visual Studio App Center:** App Center provides cross-platform crash reporting and remote debugging for mobile apps built with Xamarin. It allows for continuous testing and distribution of mobile applications while keeping track of performance and issues.

---

*4. Summary of Best Practices for Error Handling and Debugging*

- **Use Specific Exceptions:** Catch and handle specific exceptions to make your error handling more precise.

- **Log Errors Effectively:** Use logging libraries to record detailed error messages, stack traces, and debugging information.
- **Use Debuggers:** Leverage IDE-based debuggers (e.g., Visual Studio, PyCharm, VS Code) to step through your code, inspect variables, and set breakpoints.
- **Handle Platform-Specific Issues:** Be aware of platform-specific exceptions and behaviors, and handle them accordingly.
- **Remote Debugging for Mobile Apps:** Use remote debugging tools for mobile platforms (Xamarin, Android, iOS) to diagnose issues that occur on actual devices.
- **Use Error Reporting Tools:** Integrate third-party error reporting tools like Sentry or Raygun to gain real-time insights into errors and crashes across multiple platforms.
- **Automate Testing and Debugging:** Incorporate automated testing frameworks and CI/CD pipelines to catch errors early and continuously test across platforms.

By adhering to these error handling and debugging best practices, you can effectively manage and resolve issues in your cross-platform applications, improving the overall quality and user experience.

# CHAPTER 14

# PERFORMANCE OPTIMIZATION ACROSS PLATFORMS

Performance optimization is a critical aspect of cross-platform development. When building applications that must run efficiently on multiple platforms (such as Windows, macOS, Linux, iOS, and Android), performance can sometimes be impacted due to platform-specific nuances, resource limitations, and cross-platform frameworks themselves. Identifying and addressing performance issues early in the development process ensures that your application delivers a smooth, responsive experience for users, regardless of the platform they're on.

In this chapter, we will explore the best practices and techniques for optimizing performance in cross-platform applications, including the identification of common performance bottlenecks, platform-specific optimization strategies, and tools you can use to monitor and address performance issues.

---

*1. Identifying Performance Bottlenecks*

Before diving into optimization techniques, it is essential to identify performance bottlenecks in your application. Common performance issues include high CPU usage, memory leaks, slow network communication, and excessive disk access.

### a. Profiling Tools

Profiling tools help you identify where your application is spending most of its time and resources. Both Python and C# provide tools for profiling your code, allowing you to measure execution times and memory consumption.

- **Python Profiling Tools:**
  - **cProfile:** Python's built-in profiler allows you to measure the performance of your Python program and identify which parts of the code consume the most time.

    ```python
    import cProfile
    cProfile.run('my_function()')
    ```

  - **memory_profiler:** Use this tool to track memory usage over time and detect memory leaks.

    ```bash
    pip install memory_profiler
    ```

- **C# Profiling Tools:**
  - **Visual Studio Profiler:** Visual Studio provides built-in profiling tools to analyze CPU and memory usage, as well as to track performance bottlenecks in C# applications.

  o **dotTrace (JetBrains Rider):** A profiling tool for .NET applications that helps identify bottlenecks in CPU, memory, and database operations.

## b. Monitoring System Resources

Use platform-specific tools to monitor CPU, memory, and disk usage in real-time. Tools like **Task Manager** (Windows), **Activity Monitor** (macOS), and **top** (Linux) can help you identify when your application is consuming more resources than expected.

- **Android/iOS Development:** Use device-specific monitoring tools such as **Android Studio Profiler** and **Xcode Instruments** for mobile applications to analyze CPU, memory, and network usage in real-time.

---

## 2. Optimizing Application Performance

Once you've identified performance bottlenecks, the next step is to address them using optimization techniques tailored to your platform and application requirements.

## a. Optimizing CPU Performance

High CPU usage can lead to a laggy or unresponsive application. Here are some strategies to reduce CPU usage:

- **Efficient Algorithms:** Ensure you are using efficient algorithms for tasks like sorting, searching, or data processing. For example, use algorithms with a lower time complexity (e.g., $O(\log n)$ instead of $O(n^2)$).

- **Asynchronous Operations:** Avoid blocking the main thread with lengthy operations like network requests or file processing. In Python, you can use the **asyncio** module, and in C#, you can use **async/await** to run I/O-bound tasks asynchronously without blocking the UI or main thread.

  o **Python Example (asyncio):**

```python
python

import asyncio

async def fetch_data():
    # Simulate a network request
    await asyncio.sleep(2)
    return "Data fetched"

asyncio.run(fetch_data())
```

  o **C# Example (async/await):**

```csharp
csharp

public        async        Task<string>
FetchDataAsync()
{
    await    Task.Delay(2000);    //
Simulate network request
    return "Data fetched";
}
```

- **Multithreading:** For CPU-bound tasks, consider using multithreading or parallel processing to take advantage of multiple cores on the machine. In Python, the **threading** or **multiprocessing** module can be used, while in C#, the **Task Parallel Library (TPL)** or **Parallel.For** can be employed.

b. Memory Optimization

Excessive memory usage can lead to slower performance and, in extreme cases, crashes. Here are several techniques for optimizing memory usage:

- **Memory Management:** Avoid memory leaks by ensuring that resources are released when no longer needed. In C#, the **using** statement ensures that disposable objects (like files or database connections) are disposed of immediately after use.
    - **C# Example:**

    ```csharp
    using (var reader = new StreamReader("file.txt"))
    {
        var content = reader.ReadToEnd();
    }
    ```

    - **Python Example:** In Python, make use of **del** to remove references to large objects that are no longer needed or use the gc.collect() method to explicitly trigger garbage collection.

    ```python
    import gc
    del large_object
    gc.collect()
    ```

125

- **Avoid Excessive Object Creation:** Frequently creating and destroying objects can put unnecessary pressure on the garbage collector and affect performance. Reuse objects when possible.
- **Use Efficient Data Structures:** Choose the appropriate data structure for your application. For instance, use **sets** for membership tests (instead of lists), or **tuples** instead of lists if the data is immutable. In C#, consider using **ArrayLists** or **LinkedLists** when working with large collections of data.

c. Disk and File I/O Optimization

Excessive disk access or inefficient file I/O operations can slow down your application, especially on mobile or embedded platforms with limited resources.

- **Use Buffering for File I/O:** Instead of performing frequent read/write operations directly, use buffered I/O (e.g., **BufferedReader** and **BufferedWriter** in Python, or **StreamReader** and **StreamWriter** in C#) to minimize disk access.
- **Asynchronous File Operations:** Just like with network operations, consider running I/O-bound tasks asynchronously, especially for applications that need to load large files or process data in the background.

d. Network Optimization

For applications that rely on network communication, optimizing data transfer and reducing latency is crucial for performance.

- **Compression:** Use compression techniques (e.g., **gzip**, **deflate**) to minimize the size of data transferred over the network. In Python, the **gzip** module can be used, and in C#, you can use the **GZipStream** class to compress data.
- **Batch Requests:** Instead of making frequent individual network requests, batch multiple requests into a single one, if possible. This reduces the overhead of establishing connections and reduces latency.
- **Caching:** Use caching mechanisms (e.g., **Redis**, **Memcached**) to store frequently accessed data locally and avoid redundant network requests.

*3. Platform-Specific Performance Considerations*

When optimizing performance for cross-platform applications, you must take into account the differences in hardware and operating system behavior across platforms. The same application may perform well on one platform but poorly on another due to these differences.

a. Mobile Performance (iOS and Android)

- **Optimize for Battery Life:** Mobile platforms are sensitive to battery usage. Avoid unnecessary background tasks, reduce excessive CPU usage, and optimize your app's network usage to conserve battery life.
- **Efficient Image and Asset Loading:** Mobile devices, especially those with lower memory, can suffer performance issues when loading large images or assets. Use image optimization techniques like resizing or compressing images before loading them into the app. Consider lazy loading for assets that aren't immediately needed.

b. Desktop Performance

- **Adapt to Different Screen Resolutions:** On desktop platforms, ensure your application adapts to various screen sizes and resolutions. Use **responsive design** principles to make sure the UI remains usable and doesn't impact performance when scaling.
- **Leverage Native Platform APIs:** On desktop systems, make use of platform-specific optimizations such as hardware acceleration (GPU rendering) for graphics-heavy applications or file system optimizations.

c. Cross-Platform Framework Optimization

While using cross-platform frameworks like **Xamarin**, **Flutter**, or **React Native**, keep in mind that certain features or components may not be as optimized as their native counterparts.

- **Use Platform-Specific Optimizations:** Most cross-platform frameworks allow you to use platform-specific code when needed. If you experience performance bottlenecks, consider implementing platform-specific optimizations while keeping the shared codebase intact.

For example:

  o **Xamarin:** Use the **Dependency Service** to implement platform-specific code for optimizing certain operations, such as accessing sensors or file I/O.

- o **Flutter:** Use **platform channels** to invoke native code from Dart when performance demands specific platform-level optimizations.

---

*4. Monitoring and Benchmarking Tools*

Once optimizations have been applied, it's essential to monitor and benchmark your application's performance across platforms to ensure that changes have the desired effect.

a. Python Monitoring Tools

- **cProfile:** Profile your code and generate reports to see where your application is spending most of its time.
- **Py-Spy:** A sampling profiler for Python applications that allows you to profile running Python programs without modifying their code.

b. C# Monitoring Tools

- **Visual Studio Profiler:** For C# applications, Visual Studio provides comprehensive performance profiling tools that can track CPU usage, memory consumption, and disk I/O.
- **dotMemory:** A memory profiler from JetBrains Rider that helps analyze memory usage, track memory leaks, and optimize resource usage.

c. Cross-Platform Monitoring Tools

- **AppDynamics:** Provides real-time performance monitoring for cross-platform applications, including mobile and web apps.
- **New Relic:** Offers end-to-end performance monitoring for cross-platform applications, tracking database queries, API calls, and server performance.

## 5. Conclusion

Performance optimization for cross-platform applications requires a comprehensive approach, including identifying performance bottlenecks, applying platform-specific optimizations, and using the right tools for debugging, profiling, and monitoring. By addressing issues such as CPU usage, memory consumption, disk I/O, and network efficiency, and leveraging platform-specific capabilities where necessary, you can ensure that your application runs smoothly and efficiently on all platforms. Regular monitoring and benchmarking will allow you to keep performance at the forefront as your application evolves.

# CHAPTER 15

# SECURITY CONSIDERATIONS IN CROSS-PLATFORM SOFTWARE

Security is a fundamental concern in all software development, but when developing cross-platform applications, there are additional complexities to consider. With applications that run across multiple platforms (Windows, macOS, Linux, Android, iOS), the attack surface increases, and each platform may introduce unique security challenges. As a developer, it's important to follow secure coding practices and be aware of platform-specific security considerations to mitigate risks.

In this chapter, we will discuss secure coding practices, common security vulnerabilities, and platform-specific security concerns in Python and C# applications.

---

## 1. Secure Coding Practices

Regardless of the platform, secure coding practices are essential to prevent security vulnerabilities. These practices help protect your application from common attacks such as injection attacks, data leakage, and unauthorized access.

a. Input Validation and Sanitization

One of the most common sources of security vulnerabilities is improper handling of user input. Always validate and sanitize inputs to ensure they meet expected formats and constraints.

- **Python:** Use libraries like `re` (for regular expressions) or input validation frameworks to ensure data is properly validated. For web applications, use frameworks like **Django** or **Flask**, which provide built-in validation tools.

```python
import re

def validate_email(email):
    pattern = r'^[a-zA-Z0-9_.+-]+@[a-zA-Z0-9-]+\.[a-zA-Z0-9-.]+$'
    return bool(re.match(pattern, email))
```

- **C#:** In C#, use **Data Annotations** or regular expressions to validate input. Additionally, use input validation libraries for web applications like **ASP.NET Core**'s built-in validation mechanisms.

```csharp
using System.ComponentModel.DataAnnotations;

public class User
{
    [EmailAddress]
```

```
public string Email { get; set; }
}
```

b. Secure Authentication and Authorization

Ensure that user authentication and authorization are implemented securely. Passwords should always be hashed using strong cryptographic algorithms, and sensitive data should never be stored in plaintext.

- **Python:** Use libraries like **bcrypt** or **argon2** to hash passwords securely. When working with web frameworks like **Flask** or **Django**, use their built-in authentication systems, which incorporate secure methods for password storage and session management.

```python
import bcrypt

password = b"mysecretpassword"
hashed     =     bcrypt.hashpw(password,
bcrypt.gensalt())

# Verifying the password
bcrypt.checkpw(password, hashed)
```

- **C#:** In C#, use the **ASP.NET Identity** framework for handling authentication and authorization securely. For password hashing, **bcrypt** or **PBKDF2** (via **Rfc2898DeriveBytes**) can be used.

```csharp
using System.Security.Cryptography;
```

```
var password = "mysecretpassword";
var salt = new byte[16];
using        (var       rng      =        new
RNGCryptoServiceProvider())
{
    rng.GetBytes(salt);
}

var         pbkdf2        =        new
Rfc2898DeriveBytes(password, salt, 10000);
var hash = pbkdf2.GetBytes(20);
```

c. Use of Secure Communication Protocols

Ensure that sensitive data is transmitted securely by using encryption protocols such as **TLS/SSL** for communication.

- **Python:** In Python, use the **ssl** module for implementing secure communication with servers or APIs. Ensure that all communications are encrypted using HTTPS.

```python
python

import ssl
import socket

context = ssl.create_default_context()
with
socket.create_connection(('www.example.co
m', 443)) as sock:
    with          context.wrap_socket(sock,
server_hostname='www.example.com')       as
secure_sock:
        secure_sock.sendall(b"GET        /
HTTP/1.1\r\n")
```

- **C#:** In C#, the **HttpClient** class can be configured to use HTTPS for secure communication. Additionally, use **SSL/TLS** for secure API calls.

```csharp
using System.Net.Http;

var client = new HttpClient();
client.DefaultRequestHeaders.Add("User-
Agent", "MyApp");
var          response       =           await
client.GetAsync("https://www.example.com"
);
```

d. Avoiding Hard-Coding Sensitive Information

Never hard-code sensitive information such as passwords, API keys, or database connection strings directly in the source code. Use environment variables or secure vaults to store sensitive information.

- **Python:** Use environment variables to store sensitive data, and the **python-dotenv** library to load variables from a .env file.

```bash
export DB_PASSWORD="secretpassword"
python

from dotenv import load_dotenv
import os

load_dotenv()
db_password = os.getenv("DB_PASSWORD")
```

- **C#:** Use environment variables or **Azure Key Vault** to store sensitive data securely. In ASP.NET Core, **appsettings.json** can be used in combination with secret management services.

```json
json

{
   "ConnectionStrings": {
      "DefaultConnection":
"Server=myServerAddress;Database=myDataBa
se;User
Id=myUsername;Password=myPassword;"
   }
}
```

e. Avoiding Insecure Dependencies

Third-party libraries and dependencies can introduce vulnerabilities into your application. Ensure that libraries are updated regularly, and always verify their source and security.

- **Python:** Use tools like **pip-audit** or **Safety** to check for insecure dependencies in your Python project.

```bash
bash

pip install safety
safety check
```

- **C#:** In C#, use **NuGet** to manage dependencies and ensure that you're using secure, up-to-date versions of libraries. Tools like **OWASP Dependency-Check** can be used to detect known vulnerabilities.

136

## 2. Platform-Specific Security Concerns

While secure coding practices apply across all platforms, there are platform-specific security concerns that developers need to be aware of when building cross-platform applications.

### a. Security Considerations on Mobile (iOS and Android)

- **iOS:** iOS applications need to adhere to Apple's security guidelines, such as data encryption using **Keychain** and securing sensitive data stored on the device.
  - o **Keychain Services** for storing passwords and sensitive data securely.
  - o **App Transport Security (ATS)** to enforce secure connections.

```swift
let    keychain    =    Keychain(service:
"com.example.myapp")
keychain["password"] = "secret"
```

- **Android:** Android apps need to use **Keystore** for storing cryptographic keys and ensuring secure storage of sensitive information. Additionally, always enforce **Secure Network Communication (HTTPS)** for data transmission.
  - o **Android Keystore System** for securely storing cryptographic keys.

137

- Network Security Configuration to enforce the use of HTTPS.

```java
KeyStore          keyStore          =
KeyStore.getInstance("AndroidKeyStore");
keyStore.load(null);
```

b. Security Considerations on Desktop (Windows, macOS, Linux)

- **Windows:** Windows applications often face unique security challenges, such as handling **Windows Defender** and **UAC (User Account Control)**. Use the **Windows Data Protection API (DPAPI)** for secure storage of sensitive data.
  - **Windows DPAPI** to securely store application data such as passwords or connection strings.
- **macOS:** macOS applications need to leverage **Keychain Services** for secure data storage and implement **App Sandbox** to limit access to system resources.
  - **Keychain Services** for storing passwords securely.
  - **App Sandbox** to restrict access to sensitive system resources.
- **Linux:** Linux security is typically handled through **AppArmor** or **SELinux**. Developers need to ensure their applications follow best practices for file and resource permissions.

## 3. Secure Data Handling and Encryption

For cross-platform applications, secure data handling and encryption are fundamental to protecting sensitive user data both at rest and in transit.

### a. Data Encryption at Rest

Always encrypt sensitive data when stored on the device or server to prevent unauthorized access.

- **Python:** Use the **cryptography** library to encrypt and decrypt data at rest.

```python
from cryptography.fernet import Fernet

key = Fernet.generate_key()
cipher_suite = Fernet(key)
encrypted_data = cipher_suite.encrypt(b"My
sensitive data")
```

- **C#:** Use the **AesManaged** class or **RSA encryption** for encrypting data at rest in C#.

```csharp
using (Aes aesAlg = Aes.Create())
{
    aesAlg.Key = key;
    aesAlg.IV = iv;
    ICryptoTransform    encryptor    =
aesAlg.CreateEncryptor(aesAlg.Key,
aesAlg.IV);
```

```
    // Encrypt the data...
}
```

b. Data Encryption in Transit

Use **SSL/TLS** for encrypting data in transit between your application and servers to prevent eavesdropping and tampering.

- **Python:** Use **requests** library with `https` for secure communication.

  ```python
  import requests
  response                                    =
  requests.get("https://example.com")
  ```

- **C#:** Use **HttpClient** to ensure secure communication with HTTPS.

  ```csharp
  HttpClient client = new HttpClient();
  client.DefaultRequestHeaders.Add("User-
  Agent", "MyApp");
  HttpResponseMessage response = await
  client.GetAsync("https://www.example.com"
  );
  ```

*4. Conclusion*

Security is an ongoing process that must be prioritized throughout the development lifecycle, especially for cross-platform applications. Following secure coding practices, addressing platform-specific security concerns, and utilizing robust encryption techniques can significantly reduce the risk of vulnerabilities. Always ensure that your application adheres to platform-specific security standards while maintaining consistency in your security practices across platforms. By staying vigilant, performing regular security audits, and keeping dependencies up-to-date, you can protect your users and their data from evolving threats.

# CHAPTER 16

# BUILDING COMMAND-LINE APPLICATIONS IN PYTHON

Command-line applications are an essential part of software development, especially for automation, system administration, and development tasks. They provide a simple, efficient, and often faster interface for interacting with an application or performing operations. In Python, building command-line tools is straightforward thanks to its rich ecosystem of libraries and built-in support for command-line interfaces (CLI).

In this chapter, we will explore real-world examples of building efficient and robust command-line tools in Python, covering key concepts, libraries, and best practices.

---

*1. Basics of Building Command-Line Applications*

A command-line application in Python typically involves:

- **Taking input** from the user, often in the form of command-line arguments or input prompts.
- **Processing the input**, which may involve calculations, data manipulation, or file operations.
- **Providing output** to the user, either in the terminal or via files.

142

Python's built-in **argparse** library is commonly used to handle command-line arguments and make the tool more user-friendly by parsing inputs, providing help messages, and managing errors.

Example 1: Basic Command-Line Calculator

Let's start by building a simple command-line calculator that adds two numbers passed as arguments.

```python
import argparse

# Function to add two numbers
def add(a, b):
    return a + b

# Setting up the argument parser
def main():
    parser = argparse.ArgumentParser(description="A simple command-line calculator.")
    parser.add_argument('num1', type=int, help="First number")
    parser.add_argument('num2', type=int, help="Second number")
    args = parser.parse_args()

    result = add(args.num1, args.num2)
    print(f"The result of adding {args.num1} and {args.num2} is {result}")

if __name__ == '__main__':
    main()
```

How it works:

1. **argparse.ArgumentParser()**: Creates a new parser that handles command-line arguments.
2. **add()**: A simple function that performs addition.
3. **add_argument()**: Adds arguments (in this case, num1 and num2) that the user will provide via the command line.
4. **parse_args()**: Parses the arguments and stores them in args, which is an object containing the values of num1 and num2.
5. **Output**: The result of the addition is printed to the console.

Usage:
bash

```
$ python calculator.py 10 20
The result of adding 10 and 20 is 30
```

*2. Handling Complex Arguments*

For more advanced command-line applications, you may need to handle optional arguments, flags, and even subcommands. The argparse library allows you to define optional flags (like --verbose) and handle complex input scenarios.

Example 2: Command-Line Tool with Optional Arguments and Flags

Let's extend the previous calculator to support a flag for more detailed output and allow subtraction as well as addition.

```python
import argparse

def add(a, b):
    return a + b

def subtract(a, b):
    return a - b

def main():
    parser = argparse.ArgumentParser(description="A calculator that can add and subtract.")

    # Add positional arguments
    parser.add_argument('num1', type=int, help="First number")
    parser.add_argument('num2', type=int, help="Second number")

    # Add optional argument for operation
    parser.add_argument('--operation', choices=['add', 'subtract'], default='add', help="Operation to perform")

    # Add flag for verbose output
    parser.add_argument('--verbose', action='store_true', help="Show detailed output")
```

145

```
args = parser.parse_args()

if args.operation == 'add':
    result = add(args.num1, args.num2)
elif args.operation == 'subtract':
    result = subtract(args.num1, args.num2)

if args.verbose:
    print(f"Performing      {args.operation}
operation on {args.num1} and {args.num2}...")

    print(f"The result is {result}")

if __name__ == '__main__':
    main()
```

How it works:

- **choices**: Limits the value of the --operation argument to either add or subtract.
- **store_true**: The --verbose flag doesn't require a value. If the flag is passed, the corresponding value in args.verbose will be True.
- **Detailed output**: If the user passes the --verbose flag, additional information is printed.

Usage:
bash

```
$ python calculator.py 10 5 --operation subtract
The result is 5

$ python calculator.py 10 5 --operation add --
verbose
Performing add operation on 10 and 5...
The result is 15
```

### 3. Working with Files in Command-Line Applications

Many command-line applications need to process files, whether for reading input or outputting results. Python provides powerful libraries for working with files, such as **os, shutil**, and **pathlib**. We'll build an example that reads a text file, processes its content, and writes the output to another file.

Example 3: A Command-Line Tool to Count Word Frequency in a File
python

```python
import argparse
from collections import Counter
import os

def count_words(file_path):
    """Count word frequency in a text file."""
    with open(file_path, 'r') as file:
        text = file.read()
    words = text.split()
    return Counter(words)

def main():
    parser                              =
argparse.ArgumentParser(description="Count  word
frequency in a text file.")
    parser.add_argument('file',         type=str,
help="Path to the text file")
    parser.add_argument('--output',     type=str,
help="Output file to save word counts")

    args = parser.parse_args()
```

147

```python
    if not os.path.exists(args.file):
        print(f"Error: The file {args.file} does
not exist.")
        return

    word_count = count_words(args.file)

    if args.output:
        with    open(args.output,    'w')    as
output_file:
            for    word,    count    in
word_count.items():
                output_file.write(f"{word}:
{count}\n")
        print(f"Word    counts    written    to
{args.output}")
    else:
        for word, count in word_count.items():
            print(f"{word}: {count}")

if __name__ == '__main__':
    main()
```

How it works:

- **Counter**: The `collections.Counter` is used to count the frequency of each word in the file.
- **os.path.exists()**: Checks if the file exists before processing.
- **File Handling**: If the `--output` flag is used, the word counts are written to the specified output file; otherwise, the results are printed to the console.

Usage:
bash

```bash
$ python word_counter.py input.txt
```

```
hello: 3
world: 2
this: 1

$  python  word_counter.py  input.txt  --output
output.txt
Word counts written to output.txt
```

---

*4. Advanced Features: Subcommands*

For more complex command-line applications, subcommands allow you to organize functionality into different groups. For example, a command-line tool for file management might have subcommands for ing, moving, and deleting files.

Example 4: Command-Line Tool with Subcommands

Let's create a simple file management tool with subcommands for ing and moving files.

python

```
import argparse
import shutil
import os

def _file(src, dest):
    try:
        shutil.(src, dest)
        print(f"File   copied   from   {src}   to
{dest}")
    except FileNotFoundError:
        print(f"Error: {src} not found.")
    except PermissionError:
```

```
        print(f"Error: Permission denied while
ing {src}.")

def move_file(src, dest):
    try:
        shutil.move(src, dest)
        print(f"File moved from {src} to {dest}")
    except FileNotFoundError:
        print(f"Error: {src} not found.")
    except PermissionError:
        print(f"Error: Permission denied while
moving {src}.")

def main():
    parser                                    =
argparse.ArgumentParser(description="File
management tool")
    subparsers                                =
parser.add_subparsers(dest='command')

    # Subcommand for ing files
    _parser = subparsers.add_parser('', help=' a
file')
    _parser.add_argument('src',          type=str,
help="Source file path")
    _parser.add_argument('dest',         type=str,
help="Destination file path")

    # Subcommand for moving files
    move_parser = subparsers.add_parser('move',
help='Move a file')
    move_parser.add_argument('src',      type=str,
help="Source file path")
    move_parser.add_argument('dest',     type=str,
help="Destination file path")

    args = parser.parse_args()
```

```
    if args.command == '':
        _file(args.src, args.dest)
    elif args.command == 'move':
        move_file(args.src, args.dest)
    else:
        parser.print_help()

if __name__ == '__main__':
    main()
```

How it works:

- **Subcommands:** Using `subparsers`, the application can handle different subcommands (e.g., , `move`).
- **Functionality:** Based on the subcommand chosen, the appropriate function is executed (either `_file` or `move_file`).

Usage:
bash

```
$ python file_manager.py myfile.txt
/path/to/destination
File copied from myfile.txt to
/path/to/destination

$ python file_manager.py move myfile.txt
/new/path
File moved from myfile.txt to /new/path
```

---

*5. Conclusion*

Building command-line applications in Python is an effective way to create powerful, scriptable tools for automating tasks, processing data, and managing files. Python's **argparse** library offers a simple yet flexible way to handle user input, while libraries like **shutil** and **os** make it easy to interact with files and directories.

In this chapter, we covered:

- Creating basic command-line tools with input validation.
- Adding optional arguments and flags.
- Processing and writing data to files.
- Organizing functionality using subcommands.

By following these practices, you can build efficient, user-friendly command-line tools in Python that work seamlessly across different platforms, making them powerful and versatile for various use cases.

# CHAPTER 17

# CREATING GRAPHICAL USER INTERFACES IN C#

Building graphical user interfaces (GUIs) is a key part of modern software development. For cross-platform applications, you want to ensure that the UI works smoothly and looks consistent across all the platforms your application targets. C# provides several powerful frameworks for building cross-platform GUIs, with **Xamarin** and **.NET MAUI** being two of the most prominent ones for mobile, desktop, and even web applications.

In this chapter, we'll guide you through creating cross-platform GUI applications using **C#**, focusing on **Xamarin** and **.NET MAUI** (Multi-platform App UI). These frameworks help you build applications that work on Android, iOS, macOS, and Windows, leveraging a shared codebase to reduce the need for platform-specific UI implementations.

---

*1. Introduction to Xamarin and .NET MAUI*

a. Xamarin Overview

Xamarin is a framework for building cross-platform mobile applications using C# and .NET. Xamarin provides access to native APIs on Android and iOS, allowing developers to build fully native applications with a single C# codebase. It allows you to share most of your code, including business logic and UI code, across platforms.

- **Key Features of Xamarin:**
  - o **Native Performance**: Xamarin apps compile into native code, ensuring performance comparable to that of native applications.
  - o **Shared Codebase**: You can write most of your application's code in C# and share it across platforms, with platform-specific code only for features unique to a given platform.
  - o **Xamarin.Forms**: A UI toolkit that allows you to create a shared UI across platforms, while still accessing platform-specific features and controls.

b. .NET MAUI Overview

.NET MAUI is the evolution of Xamarin.Forms. It is a unified, cross-platform framework for building native applications for Android, iOS, macOS, and Windows with a single codebase. .NET MAUI is part of the .NET ecosystem and provides more modern tools and capabilities for building cross-platform desktop and mobile apps.

- **Key Features of .NET MAUI:**
  - o **Unified APIs**: .NET MAUI simplifies the development process by providing a unified API across multiple platforms.
  - o **Single Project**: Unlike Xamarin, which requires platform-specific projects, .NET MAUI uses a single project to target all platforms, reducing complexity.

- o **Cross-Platform Controls**: MAUI includes built-in controls like **Buttons**, **Labels**, and **Entry** fields that adapt to the platform's native appearance.
- o **Blazor Support**: .NET MAUI allows you to build hybrid apps using **Blazor**, enabling you to use web technologies (HTML, CSS, JavaScript) within your mobile or desktop application.

*2. Setting Up the Development Environment*

a. Installing Xamarin

1. **Install Visual Studio:**
   - o Xamarin is integrated into Visual Studio. You can install Visual Studio for free with the **Community Edition** or use the paid **Professional** or **Enterprise** editions. Make sure to select the **Mobile development with .NET** workload during installation.
2. **Xamarin Projects in Visual Studio:**
   - o Once Visual Studio is installed, create a new project and select **Mobile App (Xamarin.Forms)**. This will allow you to start building cross-platform mobile applications using Xamarin.

b. Installing .NET MAUI

1. **Install Visual Studio 2022:**
   - o .NET MAUI requires Visual Studio 2022 (version 17.3 or higher). Download and install **Visual Studio 2022**, ensuring that you select the

**.NET Multi-platform App UI development** workload during the installation.

2. **Create a .NET MAUI Project:**
   o After installation, you can create a new .NET MAUI project by selecting **.NET MAUI App** from the project templates in Visual Studio.

---

### 3. Building a Simple Cross-Platform Application with Xamarin

Let's create a simple Xamarin.Forms application that displays a greeting message on both Android and iOS.

a. Define the Shared UI
csharp

```csharp
using Xamarin.Forms;

namespace CrossPlatformApp
{
    public class MainPage : ContentPage
    {
        public MainPage()
        {
            var label = new Label
            {
                Text = "Hello, Cross-Platform World!",
                HorizontalOptions =
LayoutOptions.Center,
                VerticalOptions =
LayoutOptions.CenterAndExpand
            };

            Content = new StackLayout
            {
```

```
              Children = { label }
          };
     }
  }
}
```

b. Define Platform-Specific Configuration

In Xamarin, platform-specific code can be added when needed. For instance, you might want to change the appearance of the label on Android versus iOS. You can use **dependency services** or platform-specific code to handle this.

csharp

```
// In your Android-specific code:
[assembly:
Dependency(typeof(AndroidSpecificLabel))]
namespace CrossPlatformApp.Droid
{
    public    class    AndroidSpecificLabel    :
ILabelStyle
    {
        public string GetLabelText()
        {
            return "Hello from Android!";
        }
    }
}
```

c. Run the App

Once you have written the shared UI and platform-specific code, you can deploy your app to an Android or iOS emulator (or real device) directly from Visual Studio.

Xamarin compiles the app for the selected platform, ensuring that the app runs natively.

---

*4. Building a Simple Cross-Platform Application with .NET MAUI*

.NET MAUI simplifies cross-platform development even further by providing a unified codebase for all platforms. Here's how to build a simple .NET MAUI app that displays a greeting message.

a. Define the Shared UI
csharp

```csharp
using Microsoft.Maui.Controls;

namespace CrossPlatformApp
{
    public class MainPage : ContentPage
    {
        public MainPage()
        {
            var label = new Label
            {
                Text = "Hello, .NET MAUI World!",
                HorizontalOptions           =
LayoutOptions.Center,
                VerticalOptions             =
LayoutOptions.CenterAndExpand
            };

            Content = new StackLayout
            {
                Children = { label }
            };
        }
```

```
        }
}
```

b. Single Project Structure

With .NET MAUI, you no longer need separate projects for Android, iOS, and Windows. All platform-specific code is contained within a single project using conditional compilation, platform checks, and platform-specific APIs if necessary.

c. Run the App

Once you have written the shared UI, you can easily target multiple platforms, including Android, iOS, macOS, and Windows, by deploying the app to an emulator or device directly from Visual Studio. .NET MAUI automatically handles platform-specific optimizations and ensures a consistent UI across platforms.

---

5. Handling Platform-Specific Functionality in Xamarin and .NET MAUI

Both Xamarin and .NET MAUI provide ways to interact with platform-specific APIs and functionality. Here's how to handle common platform-specific scenarios in cross-platform applications:

a. Accessing Platform-Specific Features

For instance, if you want to access the device's camera in a cross-platform application, you can use a dependency service or platform-specific code in Xamarin and .NET MAUI.

- **Xamarin:** Use the `DependencyService` to call platform-specific code for accessing the camera on Android and iOS.

```csharp
// Define a dependency interface
public interface ICameraService
{
    void OpenCamera();
}

// Android implementation
[assembly:
Dependency(typeof(CameraServiceDroid))]
namespace CrossPlatformApp.Droid
{
    public     class     CameraServiceDroid     :
ICameraService
    {
        public void OpenCamera()
        {
            // Android-specific camera access
code
        }
    }
}

// iOS implementation
[assembly: Dependency(typeof(CameraServiceiOS))]
namespace CrossPlatformApp.iOS
{
    public     class     CameraServiceiOS     :
ICameraService
```

```
{
    public void OpenCamera()
    {
        // iOS-specific camera access code
    }
}
}
```

- **.NET MAUI:** With .NET MAUI, platform-specific functionality is easier to implement with a simple API. You can use conditional platform code to access device APIs.

csharp

```
#if ANDROID
    // Android-specific code
#elif IOS
    // iOS-specific code
#elif WINDOWS
    // Windows-specific code
#endif
```

b. Platform-Specific UI Adjustments

While both Xamarin and .NET MAUI allow you to define shared UI components, sometimes you'll need to adjust the UI for platform-specific design patterns or behaviors.

- **Xamarin:** You can use **Xamarin.Forms** to provide shared controls, but you can also apply platform-specific customizations using the **Device.OnPlatform** method or creating custom renderers.

csharp

```
var button = new Button { Text = "Click
Me!" };

if (Device.RuntimePlatform == Device.iOS)
{
    button.BackgroundColor = Color.Red;
}
else  if  (Device.RuntimePlatform  ==
Device.Android)
{
    button.BackgroundColor = Color.Green;
}
```

- **.NET MAUI:** .NET MAUI has simplified this process, offering a **VisualStateManager** that adapts UI elements based on the platform. This allows you to define custom styles for different platforms without complex code.

---

*6. Debugging and Testing Cross-Platform Apps*

Cross-platform app development requires thorough testing to ensure the app works consistently across all platforms. Here are some tips for debugging and testing your Xamarin and .NET MAUI applications:

a. Xamarin Debugging

- Use **Visual Studio**'s debugging tools to step through your code, set breakpoints, and inspect variables.

162

- Test the app on both Android and iOS simulators/emulators to ensure compatibility and check for any platform-specific issues.

### b. .NET MAUI Debugging

- With **.NET MAUI**, debugging is streamlined through Visual Studio, which provides a unified experience for testing and debugging apps across all supported platforms.
- **Live reload** allows you to quickly see changes made to the UI and functionality without needing to restart the application.

### 7. Conclusion

Creating cross-platform GUI applications with C# is efficient and straightforward with Xamarin and .NET MAUI. Both frameworks allow you to share a significant portion of your code across platforms while still enabling platform-specific customizations and optimizations when needed.

- **Xamarin** is excellent for mobile app development, while **.NET MAUI** represents the next evolution of cross-platform development, supporting mobile and desktop applications with a more unified and simplified approach

# CHAPTER 18

# CONTINUOUS INTEGRATION AND DEPLOYMENT (CI/CD) FOR CROSS-PLATFORM PROJECTS

Continuous Integration (CI) and Continuous Deployment (CD) are essential practices in modern software development, enabling teams to automate the process of building, testing, and deploying applications. By implementing CI/CD pipelines, teams can ensure faster development cycles, consistent releases, and early detection of issues.

This chapter will guide you through setting up CI/CD pipelines for both Python and C# projects, as well as provide an example of deploying a cross-platform app using **Jenkins** or **GitLab CI**.

---

*1. Introduction to CI/CD for Cross-Platform Projects*

CI/CD for cross-platform applications involves setting up automated pipelines that:

- **Build** your application on multiple platforms (e.g., Windows, macOS, Linux).

- **Test** the application on those platforms to ensure compatibility.
- **Deploy** the application to the appropriate environments (such as staging or production) across the platforms you support.

For both **Python** and **C#** projects, the key components of a CI/CD pipeline are:

1. **Code Checkout**: Fetch the latest code from the version control system (e.g., Git).
2. **Build**: Compile and package the code for all target platforms.
3. **Test**: Run unit tests, integration tests, and platform-specific tests.
4. **Deploy**: Deploy the application to a staging or production environment.

CI/CD tools like **Jenkins** and **GitLab CI** provide robust support for automating these steps across multiple platforms, ensuring that your cross-platform project works as expected on all target environments.

---

*2. Setting Up CI/CD for Python Projects*

Python is highly flexible and can be integrated into any CI/CD system. Here's how to set up a simple CI/CD pipeline for a Python project using **GitLab CI** as an example.

a. Install Dependencies and Set Up Python Environment

In GitLab CI, the pipeline configuration is defined in a `.gitlab-ci.yml` file. This file describes the different stages (build, test, deploy) of the pipeline and the jobs that run in each stage.

Example: `.gitlab-ci.yml` for Python Project
yaml

```
stages:
  - install
  - test
  - deploy

# Job to install dependencies
install_dependencies:
  stage: install
  image: python:3.9
  script:
    - pip install -r requirements.txt

# Job to run tests
run_tests:
  stage: test
  image: python:3.9
  script:
    - pytest tests/

# Job to deploy the application
deploy:
  stage: deploy
  script:
    - echo "Deploying application..."
    - # Add your deployment commands here
  only:
```

```
    - main  # Only deploy on commits to the 'main'
branch
```

How the pipeline works:

1. **install_dependencies**: This job uses the official Python 3.9 Docker image to install the dependencies specified in `requirements.txt`.

2. **run_tests**: This job runs the test suite using `pytest` to ensure the code is functioning correctly.

3. **deploy**: This stage is where the deployment process is triggered. You can replace the `echo` command with actual deployment scripts (e.g., deploying to AWS, Docker, or Heroku).

b. GitLab Runners

To run this pipeline, GitLab uses **GitLab Runners**, which can be configured to run the pipeline on different platforms (e.g., Linux, macOS, Windows). For cross-platform testing, you would need to set up different runners for each platform.

- To run tests across different platforms, you could configure multiple jobs in the `.gitlab-ci.yml` file to use different Docker images or specific runners for macOS, Windows, or Linux environments.

---

*3. Setting Up CI/CD for C# Projects*

C# projects, especially those using **.NET Core** or **.NET MAUI**, can also benefit from CI/CD pipelines. For C# projects, we can set up a pipeline using **Jenkins**.

a. Install Dependencies and Build .NET Project

For C# projects, we typically use **Jenkins** as the CI tool. Jenkins can be set up to run tests, build the project, and deploy it to various environments.

Example: Jenkinsfile for .NET Project
groovy

```
pipeline {
    agent any

    environment {
        DOTNET_CLI_HOME = '/tmp'    // Ensuring
.NET CLI uses a proper home directory
    }

    stages {
        stage('Restore') {
            steps {
                script {
                    sh 'dotnet    restore'    //
Restore project dependencies
                }
            }
        }

        stage('Build') {
            steps {
                script {
                    sh 'dotnet build -c Release'
// Build the project in Release mode
                }
            }
        }

        stage('Test') {
```

```
            steps {
                script {
                    sh 'dotnet test'  // Run unit
tests
                }
            }
        }

        stage('Publish') {
            steps {
                script {
                    sh    'dotnet    publish    -c
Release -o publish'  // Publish the application
                }
            }
        }

        stage('Deploy') {
            steps {
                script {
                    echo              'Deploying
application...'  // Replace with your deploy
logic
                }
            }
        }
    }

    post {
        success {
            echo 'Deployment successful!'
        }
        failure {
            echo 'Deployment failed!'
        }
    }
}
```

How the Jenkins pipeline works:

1. **Restore**: This stage restores the project dependencies using `dotnet restore`.
2. **Build**: Builds the project using `dotnet build`.
3. **Test**: Runs the unit tests using `dotnet test`.
4. **Publish**: Publishes the application in Release mode to a folder.
5. **Deploy**: Deploys the application (in this case, an echo statement is used, but you can replace it with real deployment commands).

b. Jenkins Agents

Jenkins allows you to set up different agents for different platforms (e.g., Windows, Linux, macOS). To test and deploy on multiple platforms, you can assign jobs to specific agents, allowing cross-platform testing in a CI/CD pipeline.

---

*4. Deploying a Cross-Platform App Using Jenkins or GitLab CI*

Once the CI/CD pipeline is set up, you can deploy your cross-platform application to a variety of environments. Here's an example of deploying a cross-platform app using **GitLab CI** and **Jenkins**.

a. Deploying a Cross-Platform App with GitLab CI

In GitLab CI, deploying a cross-platform app can involve deploying to cloud services like **AWS**, **Azure**, or **Heroku**, or running deployment scripts on various platforms (e.g., Windows or Linux servers).

For example, to deploy to **Heroku** from GitLab CI:

1. Set up a GitLab runner that runs on Linux (for simplicity).
2. Create a **deploy** job in your `.gitlab-ci.yml` file:

```yaml
deploy:
  stage: deploy
  script:
    - git remote add heroku
https://git.heroku.com/your-app-name.git
    - git push heroku main  # Deploy to
Heroku using Git
  only:
    - main
```

b. Deploying a Cross-Platform App with Jenkins

Jenkins can be used to deploy cross-platform apps by configuring different agents for each platform (e.g., Windows, macOS, Linux) and running platform-specific deployment tasks.

1. Set up Jenkins to use different agents for each target platform (Windows, Linux, macOS).
2. Configure the **Deploy** stage in the **Jenkinsfile**:

```groovy
stage('Deploy to Production') {
    steps {
        script {
```

```
if (isUnix()) {
    // Deploy to Linux
    sh 'scp -r ./publish/
user@linux-server:/path/to/deploy'
} else {
    // Deploy to Windows
    bat '     ./publish/*
C:\\path\\to\\deploy\\'
}
}
}
}
```

This deployment job checks the platform using `isUnix()` and then deploys the application accordingly.

---

*5. Best Practices for CI/CD Pipelines in Cross-Platform Development*

To ensure that your CI/CD pipeline is efficient and effective for cross-platform projects, consider the following best practices:

- **Automate Platform-Specific Testing**: Use CI/CD pipelines to run tests on different platforms to ensure compatibility. For example, you might run unit tests on Windows, Linux, and macOS to make sure your application behaves the same on all platforms.
- **Use Docker Containers**: Docker containers can help create consistent environments for building, testing, and deploying applications, regardless of the underlying platform.

- **Parallel Jobs**: To speed up the CI/CD process, run tests or deployments in parallel on multiple platforms. Both **GitLab CI** and **Jenkins** support parallel job execution.
- **Version Control**: Always ensure that the version control system (e.g., Git) is integrated with the CI/CD pipeline to trigger builds and deployments based on commits to the repository.

*6. Conclusion*

Implementing CI/CD for cross-platform projects is crucial for maintaining a fast development cycle, ensuring the stability of your application, and improving the overall deployment process. Whether you are using **GitLab CI**, **Jenkins**, or other CI/CD tools, automating the build, test, and deployment processes is key to delivering reliable and high-quality cross-platform applications.

In this chapter, we've covered:

- How to set up CI/CD pipelines for Python and C# projects.
- An example of deploying cross-platform apps using **GitLab CI** and **Jenkins**.
- Best practices for managing cross-platform deployments and testing in CI/CD pipelines.

By following these steps and best practices, you can significantly improve the efficiency and reliability of your cross-platform projects.

# CHAPTER 19

# NETWORKING AND API DEVELOPMENT ACROSS PLATFORMS

In today's interconnected world, building robust networking capabilities and API services is critical for cross-platform applications. Whether you are creating mobile apps, desktop applications, or web apps, enabling seamless communication between platforms using RESTful APIs is a common requirement. RESTful APIs allow different platforms (e.g., Android, iOS, Windows, Linux) to communicate with each other in a standard way, using HTTP protocols.

This chapter will guide you through developing RESTful APIs, handling network communications, and ensuring that your APIs work smoothly across platforms using best practices.

---

*1. Understanding RESTful APIs*

**REST (Representational State Transfer)** is an architectural style for designing networked applications. It uses a stateless, client-server communication model and relies on standard HTTP methods such as GET, POST, PUT,

DELETE, etc. RESTful APIs allow different platforms to interact with each other over the internet using these HTTP methods.

Key Concepts of RESTful APIs:

- **Stateless:** Each request from a client contains all the information needed for the server to process it. The server does not store anything about the client session between requests.
- **Uniform Interface:** APIs should have a consistent way to interact with resources (e.g., objects or data) across different endpoints.
- **HTTP Methods:**
  - o **GET**: Retrieve data from the server.
  - o **POST**: Send data to the server to create a new resource.
  - o **PUT**: Update an existing resource on the server.
  - o **DELETE**: Remove a resource from the server.
- **JSON/XML Format:** Data is usually transferred in JSON (JavaScript Object Notation) or XML format, with JSON being the most widely used.

Example of RESTful API Communication:

1. **GET Request**: Retrieving information about a user.

```bash
GET /users/{id}
Response: {
  "id": 1,
  "name": "John Doe",
  "email": "john.doe@example.com"
}
```

## 2. POST Request: Creating a new user.

```css
css
```

```
POST /users
Request Body: {
  "name": "Jane Doe",
  "email": "jane.doe@example.com"
}
Response: {
  "id": 2,
  "name": "Jane Doe",
  "email": "jane.doe@example.com"
}
```

---

*2. Developing RESTful APIs in Python*

In Python, there are several frameworks available for building RESTful APIs, with **Flask** and **Django** being the most popular. We'll focus on **Flask**, as it's lightweight, flexible, and ideal for smaller projects.

a. Setting Up a Basic Flask API

### 1. Install Flask:

```bash
bash
```

```
pip install Flask
```

### 2. Create a Simple Flask API:

```python
python
```

```
from flask import Flask, jsonify, request
```

```python
app = Flask(__name__)

# Sample data
users = [
    {"id": 1, "name": "John Doe", "email":
"john.doe@example.com"},
    {"id": 2, "name": "Jane Doe", "email":
"jane.doe@example.com"}
]

# Endpoint to get user data
@app.route('/users', methods=['GET'])
def get_users():
    return jsonify(users)

# Endpoint to create a new user
@app.route('/users', methods=['POST'])
def create_user():
    new_user = request.get_json()
    users.append(new_user)
    return jsonify(new_user), 201

# Run the app
if __name__ == '__main__':
    app.run(debug=True)
```

How it works:

- The **GET /users** endpoint returns a list of users in JSON format.
- The **POST /users** endpoint allows creating new users by sending data in JSON format.
- **Flask** is simple to use, but can be expanded with authentication, authorization, and more complex routing logic as needed.

b. Testing the API:

You can test the API using **Postman** or **curl**:

- **GET Request (List Users):**

bash

```
curl http://127.0.0.1:5000/users
```

- **POST Request (Create User):**

bash

```
curl -X POST http://127.0.0.1:5000/users -
H "Content-Type: application/json" -d
'{"id": 3, "name": "Sam Smith", "email":
"sam.smith@example.com"}'
```

---

*3. Developing RESTful APIs in C#*

In C#, **ASP.NET Core** is the go-to framework for building robust, high-performance RESTful APIs. It's cross-platform, meaning it runs on Windows, Linux, and macOS, and it's highly scalable.

a. Setting Up a Basic ASP.NET Core Web API

1. **Install .NET SDK:**
   o If you don't already have .NET installed, you can download it from here.
2. **Create a New Web API Project:**

bash

```
dotnet new webapi -n MyApi
cd MyApi
```

## 3. Create a Simple Controller for Users:

In the `Controllers` folder, create a `UserController.cs` file:

csharp

```csharp
using Microsoft.AspNetCore.Mvc;
using System.Collections.Generic;

namespace MyApi.Controllers
{
    [Route("api/[controller]")]
    [ApiController]
    public class UsersController :
ControllerBase
    {
        private static List<User> users = new
List<User>
        {
            new User { Id = 1, Name = "John Doe",
Email = "john.doe@example.com" },
            new User { Id = 2, Name = "Jane Doe",
Email = "jane.doe@example.com" }
        };

        // GET: api/users
        [HttpGet]
        public ActionResult<List<User>>
GetUsers()
        {
            return users;
        }
```

179

```
        // POST: api/users
        [HttpPost]
        public                  ActionResult<User>
CreateUser(User user)
        {
            users.Add(user);
            return
CreatedAtAction(nameof(GetUsers),  new  {  id  =
user.Id },  user);
        }
    }

    public class User
    {
        public int Id { get; set; }
        public string Name { get; set; }
        public string Email { get; set; }
    }
}
```

b. Running and Testing the API

1. Run the API by executing:

```bash

dotnet run
```

2. Test the API using Postman or **curl**:

- **GET Request (List Users):**

```bash

curl http://localhost:5000/api/users
```

- **POST Request (Create User):**

180

```bash
bash
```

```bash
curl                -X              POST
http://localhost:5000/api/users     -H
"Content-Type:   application/json"   -d
'{"Id": 3, "Name": "Sam Smith", "Email":
"sam.smith@example.com"}'
```

*4. Handling Network Communications Between Platforms*

Once your API is up and running, you need to manage network communications between the client (e.g., mobile or desktop app) and the server (API). Both **Python** and **C#** have built-in libraries for making HTTP requests.

a. Making HTTP Requests in Python

In Python, **requests** is the most popular library for handling HTTP requests.

1. **Install Requests:**

   ```bash
   bash

   pip install requests
   ```

2. **Example of Making a GET Request:**

```python
python

import requests

response                                  =
requests.get('http://localhost:5000/api/users')
users = response.json()
```

181

```python
print(users)
```

### 3. Example of Making a POST Request:

python

```python
import requests
import json

new_user = {"id": 3, "name": "Sam Smith",
"email": "sam.smith@example.com"}
response =
requests.post('http://localhost:5000/api/users'
, json=new_user)
print(response.status_code, response.json())
```
b. Making HTTP Requests in C#

In C#, you can use **HttpClient** for making HTTP requests to APIs.

### 1. Example of Making a GET Request:

csharp

```csharp
using System;
using System.Net.Http;
using System.Threading.Tasks;

class Program
{
    static async Task Main(string[] args)
    {
        using var client = new HttpClient();
        var response = await
client.GetStringAsync("http://localhost:5000/ap
i/users");
        Console.WriteLine(response);
```

```
        }
}
```

## 2. Example of Making a POST Request:

```csharp
using System;
using System.Net.Http;
using System.Text;
using System.Threading.Tasks;

class Program
{
    static async Task Main(string[] args)
    {
        using var client = new HttpClient();
        var userJson = "{\"Id\": 3, \"Name\":
\"Sam          Smith\",           \"Email\":
\"sam.smith@example.com\"}";
        var        content        =           new
StringContent(userJson,           Encoding.UTF8,
"application/json");

        var        response        =        await
client.PostAsync("http://localhost:5000/api/use
rs", content);
        Console.WriteLine(response.StatusCode);
    }
}
```

---

*5. Cross-Platform Communication and API Security*

When handling network communications across platforms, it's essential to ensure secure communication using **HTTPS**, protect sensitive data, and authenticate requests.

## a. Using HTTPS

Ensure that all communication between the client and the server is encrypted by using **HTTPS**. Both Python and C# frameworks support HTTPS by default, but you'll need to configure your API to serve over HTTPS in production.

## b. Authentication and Authorization

For secure communication between platforms, implement authentication mechanisms like **JWT (JSON Web Tokens)** or **OAuth** to ensure that only authorized clients can access the API.

- **Python Example (JWT Authentication)**: Use the **PyJWT** library to generate and verify JWT tokens.
- **C# Example (JWT Authentication)**: Use **ASP.NET Core Identity** and **JWT Bearer Authentication** middleware to secure your API endpoints.

---

## 6. Conclusion

In this chapter, we explored how to develop and handle network communications with RESTful APIs across platforms. Key topics covered include:

- **Building RESTful APIs** in both **Python** (using **Flask**) and **C#** (using **ASP.NET Core**).
- **Handling HTTP requests** from Python and C# clients.

- Ensuring **secure communication** by implementing HTTPS, authentication, and authorization.

By understanding these concepts and applying best practices, you can develop robust, scalable, and secure cross-platform applications that effectively communicate over the network using RESTful APIs.

# CHAPTER 20

# CROSS-PLATFORM MOBILE DEVELOPMENT WITH PYTHON

Building cross-platform mobile applications is becoming increasingly popular as it allows developers to target multiple mobile platforms (Android, iOS) with a single codebase. Python, traditionally known for its use in web development, data science, and scripting, also provides frameworks for mobile app development. Two popular frameworks for building cross-platform mobile apps with Python are **Kivy** and **BeeWare**.

In this chapter, we will introduce both **Kivy** and **BeeWare**, explore their features, and guide you through building a simple mobile app with each framework.

---

*1. Introduction to Kivy*

**Kivy** is an open-source Python library for rapid development of applications with rich user interfaces. It's especially suitable for developing mobile apps as it allows you to write apps for Android, iOS, macOS, and Windows using a single codebase.

Key Features of Kivy:

- **Cross-Platform:** Kivy supports Android, iOS, Linux, macOS, and Windows.
- **User Interface (UI) Design:** Kivy provides a wide variety of UI elements and supports gestures, multi-touch, and accelerometer functionality.
- **Graphics Support:** Kivy has built-in support for OpenGL ES 2, making it ideal for graphics-heavy apps, such as games or visualizations.
- **Customizable Widgets:** It offers a wide range of customizable UI components, such as buttons, sliders, and text inputs.

Setting Up Kivy for Mobile Development

To start using Kivy, you need to install the Kivy framework and some additional dependencies for building mobile applications.

1. **Install Kivy:** First, install Kivy by running:

```bash

pip install kivy
```

2. **Install Buildozer (for Android): Buildozer** is a tool that helps package Python applications for Android. To install Buildozer:

```bash

pip install buildozer
sudo apt install build-essential cpython3-
dev python3-setuptools python3-pip
```

3. **Install Xcode (for iOS):** For iOS development, you'll need to install **Xcode** on macOS, as it provides the tools necessary for compiling the app for iOS.

Example: A Simple Kivy App

Here's how to create a simple Kivy application that displays a button. When the button is pressed, it changes the label text.

python

```python
from kivy.app import App
from kivy.uix.button import Button
from kivy.uix.label import Label
from kivy.uix.boxlayout import BoxLayout

class MyApp(App):
    def build(self):
        self.label = Label(text="Hello, World!")
        self.button = Button(text="Click Me")

self.button.bind(on_press=self.change_text)

        layout                              =
BoxLayout(orientation='vertical')
        layout.add_widget(self.label)
        layout.add_widget(self.button)

        return layout

    def change_text(self, instance):
        self.label.text = "Button Clicked!"

if __name__ == "__main__":
    MyApp().run()
```

How it works:

1. The **Button** widget is created and bound to the change_text method. When the button is pressed, it updates the **Label** widget's text.
2. **BoxLayout** is used to arrange the widgets vertically.

Running the App:

You can run the Kivy app locally on your computer using:

```bash
```

```
python main.py
```

For mobile platforms, use **Buildozer** to package and deploy your app to Android or iOS.

- **Build for Android**:

```bash
```

```
buildozer android debug
```

- **Build for iOS (on macOS)**:

```bash
```

```
buildozer ios debug
```

---

*2. Introduction to BeeWare*

**BeeWare** is another Python framework for building cross-platform mobile apps, as well as desktop and web apps.

BeeWare allows you to write mobile apps in Python and deploy them to Android and iOS. Unlike Kivy, BeeWare apps look and feel like native apps, making it a great choice for developers who want to build applications that adhere to the design guidelines of each platform.

Key Features of BeeWare:

- **Cross-Platform:** BeeWare supports Android, iOS, macOS, Linux, Windows, and even web applications.
- **Native Look and Feel:** BeeWare provides native widgets for each platform, ensuring that the app adheres to platform-specific design conventions.
- **Python-to-Native API:** BeeWare translates Python code into native code for each platform.

Setting Up BeeWare for Mobile Development

To start using BeeWare, you need to install the BeeWare toolkit, including the **Toga** library for creating cross-platform mobile apps.

1. **Install Toga:** Toga is BeeWare's library for building native UIs. Install it via pip:

bash

```
pip install toga
```

2. **Install BeeWare SDK:** For Android or iOS, you will need to install the BeeWare SDK and platform-specific build tools.
   - o For **Android**, install **Android Studio** and configure it to work with Toga.

190

o   For **iOS**, install **Xcode** on macOS.

Example: A Simple BeeWare App

Here's an example of a simple BeeWare app that creates a button, and when clicked, displays a message.

python

```python
import toga
from toga.style import Pack
from toga.style.pack import COLUMN, ROW

class MyApp(toga.App):
    def startup(self):
        # Create a box layout for the app window
        self.main_box                          =
toga.Box(style=Pack(direction=COLUMN))

        # Create a button that will call the
`say_hello` method when pressed
        self.button = toga.Button('Click Me!',
on_press=self.say_hello, style=Pack(padding=20))

        # Create a label to display a message
        self.label = toga.Label('Hello, World!',
style=Pack(padding=10))

        # Add button and label to the main box
        self.main_box.add(self.label)
        self.main_box.add(self.button)

        # Create the main window and set the
content
        self.main_window                       =
toga.MainWindow(title="BeeWare App", size=(300,
200))
```

```
    self.main_window.content = self.main_box
    self.main_window.show()

def say_hello(self, widget):
    self.label.text = "Button Clicked!"

if __name__ == '__main__':
    app    =    MyApp('My    BeeWare    App',
'org.beeware.myapp')
    app.main_loop()
```

How it works:

1.  The app creates a **Button** and a **Label**.
2.  When the button is pressed, the `say_hello` method is invoked, which updates the label text.
3.  The UI is organized in a **Box** layout with **vertical stacking**.

Running the App:

To run your BeeWare application on your local system:

bash

```
python main.py
```

For mobile platforms, you can build and deploy the app using **Briefcase**.

- **Build for Android:**

    bash

    ```
    briefcase new android
    ```

192

Follow the instructions to configure the project, then run:

```bash
briefcase package android
```

- **Build for iOS:**

```bash
briefcase new ios
```

After configuration, run:

```bash
briefcase package ios
```

---

*3. Key Differences Between Kivy and BeeWare*

While both **Kivy** and **BeeWare** are powerful frameworks for building cross-platform mobile apps with Python, there are key differences that might make you prefer one over the other based on your needs:

| Feature | Kivy | BeeWare |
|---|---|---|
| **Cross-Platform** | Android, iOS, Windows, Linux, macOS | Android, iOS, Windows, macOS, Linux, Web |

| Feature | Kivy | BeeWare |
|---|---|---|
| UI Look & Feel | Customizable, non-native | Native widgets (platform-specific) |
| Complexity | Easier to start, but more customizability required for native look | Native look but slightly more complex for mobile apps |
| Graphics Support | Built-in OpenGL support for graphics-heavy apps | Limited graphics support compared to Kivy |
| Community & Support | Large community, mature framework | Growing community, relatively newer |

- **Kivy** is ideal for developing apps that require advanced graphics or custom UI components and for those who don't need to strictly follow platform design guidelines.
- **BeeWare** is perfect for developers who want to build native-looking apps and are willing to manage more complexity for iOS and Android deployments.

---

*4. Conclusion*

Both **Kivy** and **BeeWare** are excellent choices for building cross-platform mobile applications using Python, depending on your project requirements. **Kivy** offers flexibility and is suitable for applications requiring custom UIs and graphics, while **BeeWare** is the go-to solution for building native-looking apps that adhere to platform-specific guidelines.

By leveraging these frameworks, Python developers can build powerful and responsive mobile apps that run on multiple platforms, all with a single codebase.

# CHAPTER 21

# BUILDING CROSS-PLATFORM MOBILE APPLICATIONS WITH C#

Mobile application development has evolved significantly, and cross-platform frameworks allow developers to create apps that run on multiple platforms using a single codebase. **Xamarin** is one of the most popular frameworks for building cross-platform mobile applications with C#. Xamarin enables you to write native applications for **Android, iOS**, and **Windows** using C# and the .NET ecosystem.

This chapter will provide a real-world guide to building cross-platform mobile applications with Xamarin. It will cover **UI design**, **handling device features** (like camera, geolocation, and sensors), and building functional apps with Xamarin.

---

*1. Introduction to Xamarin*

Xamarin is a framework built on top of **.NET** that allows developers to build **native cross-platform applications**. Xamarin provides access to platform-specific APIs, and its **Xamarin.Forms** module enables the development of shared user interfaces across multiple platforms (Android, iOS, and UWP). Xamarin applications are compiled into native code, which provides near-native performance.

Key Features of Xamarin:

- **Shared Codebase**: Most of the application code, including business logic and UI code, can be shared across Android, iOS, and Windows.
- **Native Performance**: Xamarin compiles the app into native code for Android and iOS, offering better performance than hybrid apps.
- **Platform-Specific Code**: For platform-specific features, Xamarin allows you to write native code when necessary.
- **Xamarin.Forms**: A UI toolkit that allows developers to create a single user interface for multiple platforms.

---

*2. Setting Up Xamarin for Cross-Platform Development*

To get started with Xamarin, you'll need to install **Visual Studio** with the **Mobile development with .NET** workload. This allows you to create Xamarin applications for Android and iOS.

Installation Steps:

1. **Install Visual Studio**:
   - Download and install **Visual Studio** (Community, Professional, or Enterprise).
   - During installation, select the **Mobile development with .NET** workload, which includes Xamarin.
2. **Set Up Android Emulator (for Android)**:
   - Android Studio provides an emulator that can be used to run Android apps from Visual Studio.
   - Install **Android Studio** and set up the emulator.
3. **Set Up iOS Simulator (for macOS)**:

o **Xcode** is required for building iOS apps on macOS. Install **Xcode** from the Mac App Store and configure it to work with Xamarin.

*3. Creating a Simple Xamarin App*

Let's create a basic Xamarin application that displays a button. When the button is clicked, it will update a label's text.

a. Creating the Project

1. Open **Visual Studio** and select **Create a new project**.
2. Choose **Mobile App (Xamarin.Forms)** and then select the **Blank App** template.

b. Building the UI with Xamarin.Forms

In **Xamarin.Forms**, the UI is defined in the `MainPage.xaml` file. Let's build a simple interface with a button and a label.

```xml
<?xml version="1.0" encoding="utf-8" ?>
<ContentPage
xmlns="http://xamarin.com/schemas/2014/forms"

xmlns:x="http://schemas.microsoft.com/winfx/200
6/xaml"

x:Class="CrossPlatformApp.MainPage">
    <StackLayout>
        <Label    x:Name="label"    Text="Hello,
Xamarin!"
```

198

```
VerticalOptions="CenterAndExpand"

HorizontalOptions="CenterAndExpand"/>
        <Button Text="Click Me!"

VerticalOptions="CenterAndExpand"

HorizontalOptions="CenterAndExpand"
                Clicked="OnButtonClicked"/>
    </StackLayout>
</ContentPage>
```

c. Implementing the Button Click in Code-Behind

Now, open the **MainPage.xaml.cs** file and implement the OnButtonClicked event handler to update the label when the button is pressed.

csharp

```csharp
using Xamarin.Forms;

namespace CrossPlatformApp
{
    public partial class MainPage : ContentPage
    {
        public MainPage()
        {
            InitializeComponent();
        }

        private    void    OnButtonClicked(object
sender, EventArgs e)
        {
            label.Text = "Button Clicked!";
        }
    }
```

```
}
```

How it works:

- **XAML File:** The `Label` and `Button` are defined in the `MainPage.xaml` file, and the layout is managed with a `StackLayout`.
- **Code-Behind (MainPage.xaml.cs):** The button click event changes the text of the label.

### d. Running the App on Android and iOS

You can run the app on an Android emulator, iOS simulator (macOS only), or real devices by selecting the target from the top toolbar in Visual Studio. Xamarin handles the build process for each platform.

---

### 4. Handling Device Features in Xamarin

Xamarin provides powerful APIs to access device features such as the camera, GPS, accelerometer, and more. You can either use **Xamarin.Essentials** (a library that simplifies common device features) or write platform-specific code when needed.

### a. Accessing the Camera

To access the camera in Xamarin, you can use the **Xamarin.Essentials** library, which abstracts away platform-specific APIs.

1. **Install Xamarin.Essentials:** Xamarin.Essentials is available through NuGet and can be installed by running:

```bash
Install-Package Xamarin.Essentials
```

2. **Add Camera Permissions:** Ensure you have the appropriate permissions to access the camera on Android and iOS:
   - **Android**: Modify the `AndroidManifest.xml` file.
   - **iOS**: Modify the `Info.plist` file.
3. **Using Xamarin.Essentials to Take a Photo:**

```csharp
using Xamarin.Essentials;
using Xamarin.Forms;

namespace CrossPlatformApp
{
    public partial class MainPage : ContentPage
    {
        public MainPage()
        {
            InitializeComponent();
        }

        private async void OnButtonClicked(object sender, EventArgs e)
        {
            var photo = await MediaPicker.CapturePhotoAsync();
```

```
            var       stream      =          await
photo.OpenReadAsync();
            label.Text    =    $"Photo      taken:
{photo.FileName}";
        }
    }
}
```

How it works:

- **CapturePhotoAsync**: The `CapturePhotoAsync` method uses the device's camera to take a photo.
- **Permissions**: Ensure you have the necessary permissions to access the camera on both Android and iOS devices.

b. Accessing Device Geolocation

You can also use **Xamarin.Essentials** to get the device's current location.

1. **Add Permissions:**
   o **Android**: Add permissions to `AndroidManifest.xml`.
   o **iOS**: Add permissions to `Info.plist`.
2. **Using Xamarin.Essentials for Geolocation:**

csharp

```
using Xamarin.Essentials;

namespace CrossPlatformApp
{
    public partial class MainPage : ContentPage
    {
        public MainPage()
        {
            InitializeComponent();
```

```
        }

        private          async          void
OnGetLocationClicked(object sender, EventArgs e)
        {
            var      location      =      await
Geolocation.GetLastKnownLocationAsync();
            if (location != null)
            {
                label.Text    =    $"Location:
{location.Latitude}, {location.Longitude}";
            }
            else
            {
                label.Text = "Unable to retrieve
location.";
            }
        }
    }
}
```

How it works:

- **GetLastKnownLocationAsync**: This method retrieves the last known location of the device, returning latitude and longitude.

c. Handling Accelerometer Data

You can access the device's accelerometer to measure movement using Xamarin.Essentials.

csharp

```
using Xamarin.Essentials;

namespace CrossPlatformApp
{
```

203

```
public partial class MainPage : ContentPage
{
    public MainPage()
    {
        InitializeComponent();
    }

    private                              void
OnStartAccelerometerClicked(object       sender,
EventArgs e)
    {
        Accelerometer.ReadingChanged     +=
Accelerometer_ReadingChanged;

Accelerometer.Start(SensorSpeed.UI);
    }

    private                              void
Accelerometer_ReadingChanged(object      sender,
AccelerometerChangedEventArgs e)
    {
        label.Text  =  $"Acceleration  X:
{e.Reading.Acceleration.X},              Y:
{e.Reading.Acceleration.Y},              Z:
{e.Reading.Acceleration.Z}";
    }
}
}
```

How it works:

- **Accelerometer.ReadingChanged**: The
  ReadingChanged event is triggered whenever the
  accelerometer's readings change.
- **SensorSpeed.UI**: The sensor updates at a speed suitable
  for UI interaction.

## 5. Deploying the App

To deploy your Xamarin app to the App Store (iOS) or Google Play (Android), you need to package and sign the app appropriately.

- **Android**: Use **Buildozer** or **Visual Studio** to create an APK file and sign it for distribution on Google Play.
- **iOS**: Use **Xcode** to create an IPA file, sign it with an Apple Developer certificate, and deploy it on the App Store.

## 6. Conclusion

In this chapter, we explored how to build cross-platform mobile applications using **Xamarin**, a powerful C# framework for building native mobile apps for Android and iOS. Key topics covered include:

- **Building UIs with Xamarin.Forms**: Creating shared UI for multiple platforms.
- **Accessing device features**: Using **Xamarin.Essentials** to access the camera, geolocation, and accelerometer.
- **Handling platform-specific functionality**: Writing code for platform-specific features when necessary.

Xamarin allows C# developers to build high-performance, native mobile applications with shared code for multiple platforms. By following these steps and utilizing Xamarin's extensive libraries and tools, you can create fully-featured, cross-platform mobile apps that meet modern requirements.

# CHAPTER 22

# CONCURRENCY AND PARALLELISM IN PYTHON AND C#

Concurrency and parallelism are fundamental concepts in modern software development, especially when building **cross-platform applications** that need to perform multiple tasks simultaneously or handle heavy computational loads efficiently. By leveraging these concepts, you can improve the performance and responsiveness of your applications.

In this chapter, we will explore advanced concepts in **parallel programming** and **asynchronous operations** for both **Python** and **C#**. We will look at how to implement concurrency and parallelism in cross-platform software, including key techniques and tools to optimize execution on multiple platforms (Windows, Linux, macOS, Android, and iOS).

---

*1. Understanding Concurrency and Parallelism*

Before diving into implementation, it's important to understand the difference between concurrency and parallelism:

- **Concurrency** refers to the ability to handle multiple tasks at once, but not necessarily simultaneously. It's about managing multiple tasks in a way that makes progress, often by switching between tasks quickly (e.g., multitasking in operating systems).
- **Parallelism** involves performing multiple tasks simultaneously, usually with multiple processors or cores. It's an extension of concurrency where multiple tasks are executed at the same time.

For **cross-platform development**, both concurrency and parallelism are important to improve the performance of your applications, especially on multi-core systems or mobile devices.

---

## 2. Concurrency and Asynchronous Programming in Python

Python provides several libraries and mechanisms to handle concurrency and asynchronous programming. The two most commonly used approaches for handling concurrency in Python are **threads** and **asyncio**.

### a. Using Threads for Concurrency

Python's **threading** module allows you to run multiple threads concurrently in a program. Threads are lightweight and share the same memory space, which allows for quick context switching but may lead to issues like race conditions if not handled properly.

## Example: Using Threading in Python

```python
python

import threading
import time

# Function to simulate a task
def task(name, delay):
    print(f"Task {name} started")
    time.sleep(delay)
    print(f"Task {name} completed")

# Creating threads
thread1     =     threading.Thread(target=task,
args=("A", 2))
thread2     =     threading.Thread(target=task,
args=("B", 3))

# Starting threads
thread1.start()
thread2.start()

# Wait for both threads to finish
thread1.join()
thread2.join()

print("Both tasks completed.")
```

How it works:

- Two threads are created to run the `task` function concurrently. Each thread will sleep for a different amount of time, simulating a task that takes time to complete.
- **join()** is used to wait for the threads to finish before proceeding.

b. Using Asyncio for Concurrency

The **asyncio** library in Python is designed for writing asynchronous, non-blocking code using the `async/await` syntax. It allows you to handle many tasks concurrently without the need for threads.

**Example: Using Asyncio in Python**

python

```python
import asyncio

# Function to simulate an async task
async def task(name, delay):
    print(f"Task {name} started")
    await asyncio.sleep(delay)
    print(f"Task {name} completed")

# Running multiple async tasks concurrently
async def main():
    # Start tasks concurrently
    await asyncio.gather(task("A", 2), task("B", 3))

# Running the event loop
asyncio.run(main())
```

How it works:

- **async def**: Defines an asynchronous function.
- **await**: Used to yield control back to the event loop while waiting for an operation to complete (e.g., `sleep`).
- **asyncio.gather()**: Runs multiple asynchronous tasks concurrently.

c. Using Multiprocessing for Parallelism in Python

For CPU-bound tasks, Python's **multiprocessing** module is ideal because it bypasses the Global Interpreter Lock (GIL) and runs each process in its own memory space, enabling true parallelism.

## Example: Using Multiprocessing in Python

```python
import multiprocessing

# Function to simulate a CPU-bound task
def cpu_task(name, count):
    result = sum(i for i in range(count))
    print(f"Task {name} result: {result}")

# Creating processes
process1                                        =
multiprocessing.Process(target=cpu_task,
args=("A", 1000000))
process2                                        =
multiprocessing.Process(target=cpu_task,
args=("B", 1000000))

# Starting processes
process1.start()
process2.start()

# Wait for both processes to finish
process1.join()
process2.join()

print("Both CPU-bound tasks completed.")
```

How it works:

- **multiprocessing.Process** creates separate processes for each task, running them concurrently on different CPU cores.
- Each process executes independently and in parallel.

---

*3. Concurrency and Asynchronous Programming in C#*

In C#, you can achieve concurrency using **async/await** (for asynchronous programming) and **threads or tasks** (for concurrent or parallel execution). C# also provides tools for parallel execution through **Parallel.For**, **Task Parallel Library (TPL)**, and **async/await** for asynchronous programming.

a. Using Async/Await for Concurrency in C#

C# provides the `async` and `await` keywords to perform asynchronous programming. This helps in executing I/O-bound tasks without blocking the main thread.

**Example: Using Async/Await in C#**

csharp

```
using System;
using System.Threading.Tasks;

class Program
{
    // Async method to simulate an asynchronous
task
```

211

```
    static async Task TaskAsync(string name, int
delay)
    {
        Console.WriteLine($"Task          {name}
started.");
        await  Task.Delay(delay  *  1000);    //
Simulate async work
        Console.WriteLine($"Task          {name}
completed.");
    }

    static async Task Main(string[] args)
    {
        // Start tasks concurrently
        await Task.WhenAll(
            TaskAsync("A", 2),
            TaskAsync("B", 3)
        );

        Console.WriteLine("Both            tasks
completed.");
    }
}
```

How it works:

- **Task.Delay()** simulates an asynchronous operation (e.g., a web request).
- **Task.WhenAll()** waits for multiple asynchronous tasks to complete.

b. Using Parallelism in C# with the Task Parallel Library (TPL)

For CPU-bound tasks, you can use the **Task Parallel Library (TPL)** or **Parallel.For** to parallelize the work.

**Example: Using Parallel.For in C#**

```csharp

using System;
using System.Threading.Tasks;

class Program
{
    static void Main()
    {
        // Parallel execution of CPU-bound tasks
        Parallel.For(0, 5, i =>
        {
            Console.WriteLine($"Task    {i}    is
being         processed        on           thread
{System.Threading.Thread.CurrentThread.ManagedT
hreadId}");
        });

        Console.WriteLine("All    parallel    tasks
completed.");
    }
}
```

How it works:

- **Parallel.For** runs the loop iterations in parallel on multiple threads.
- Each task runs concurrently on different threads, leveraging multiple CPU cores.

c. Using Threads for Concurrency in C#

While TPL and `async/await` are the modern approach for parallelism, you can also use **threads** to perform concurrent work.

**Example: Using Threads in C#**

```
csharp

using System;
using System.Threading;

class Program
{
    static void TaskMethod(string name)
    {
        Console.WriteLine($"{name}  is  starting
on                                        thread
{Thread.CurrentThread.ManagedThreadId}");
        Thread.Sleep(2000); // Simulate work
        Console.WriteLine($"{name}                is
finished.");
    }

    static void Main()
    {
        // Create  two  threads  to  run  tasks
concurrently
        Thread  thread1  =  new  Thread(()  =>
TaskMethod("Task 1"));
        Thread  thread2  =  new  Thread(()  =>
TaskMethod("Task 2"));

        thread1.Start();
        thread2.Start();

        thread1.Join();
        thread2.Join();

        Console.WriteLine("Both              tasks
completed.");
    }
}
```

How it works:

- **Thread** starts a new thread to run a task concurrently.
- **Join** ensures that the main thread waits for the threads to finish before exiting.

---

*4. Performance Considerations*

When implementing concurrency and parallelism, there are several performance considerations:

- **Thread Overhead**: Each thread has its own memory space and context, which incurs some overhead. If you are working with a large number of threads, this can become costly.
- **Synchronization**: When working with threads, you may need to manage shared resources (e.g., shared variables or memory). Use synchronization techniques like **locks** or **mutexes** to avoid race conditions and data corruption.
- **CPU vs. I/O Bound**: For **I/O-bound tasks** (e.g., making API calls or reading from disk), use asynchronous programming with `async/await`. For **CPU-bound tasks**, consider parallelism or multiprocessing for better performance.
- **Thread Pool**: Both C# and Python allow you to use a **thread pool** (via **ThreadPool** in C# and **concurrent.futures** in Python) to reuse threads instead of creating new ones, which can help reduce overhead.

215

*5. Conclusion*

Concurrency and parallelism are critical for optimizing the performance of cross-platform applications, especially when dealing with I/O-bound and CPU-bound operations. By leveraging **async/await**, **threads**, **tasks**, and the **Task Parallel Library (TPL)**, both **Python** and **C#** allow you to build scalable and efficient applications.

In this chapter, we covered:

- **Concurrency** in Python using `asyncio` and `threading`.
- **Parallelism** in Python using `multiprocessing`.
- **Concurrency** in C# using **async/await** and **Threads**.
- **Parallelism** in C# using the **Task Parallel Library (TPL)** and **Parallel.For**.

By understanding and applying these concepts effectively, you can significantly enhance the performance and responsiveness of your cross-platform software.

# CHAPTER 23

# TESTING STRATEGIES FOR CROSS-PLATFORM APPLICATIONS

Testing is one of the most critical aspects of software development, especially when building cross-platform applications. With a diverse range of platforms and devices, ensuring that your application works seamlessly across all supported environments is a challenge that requires a robust testing strategy. This chapter will explore how to write and run **cross-platform tests** using popular **Python** and **C#** **testing frameworks**, ensuring your application's reliability, stability, and performance across all platforms (e.g., Windows, macOS, Linux, Android, iOS).

---

*1. Importance of Cross-Platform Testing*

Cross-platform testing ensures that your application works consistently across various operating systems, devices, and screen sizes. The goal is to detect and fix issues before the application reaches the users, providing a smooth experience no matter the platform.

Key Testing Types for Cross-Platform Apps:

- **Unit Testing**: Tests individual functions or methods to ensure they behave as expected.
- **Integration Testing**: Verifies that different parts of the system work together correctly.
- **UI/Functional Testing**: Ensures the user interface behaves as expected across different devices and screen sizes.
- **End-to-End (E2E) Testing**: Tests the entire flow of the application from start to finish, simulating user behavior.
- **Performance Testing**: Measures the responsiveness and stability of the application under different conditions.

---

*2. Testing Strategies in Python*

In Python, several testing frameworks and tools are available to help you write and execute tests. The most commonly used testing libraries for Python are **unittest**, **pytest**, and **Selenium** for UI testing.

a. Unit Testing with unittest

**unittest** is Python's built-in testing framework and is suitable for writing unit tests and integration tests.

**Example: Writing Unit Tests with unittest**

```python
import unittest

def add(a, b):
```

```
    return a + b

class TestMathOperations(unittest.TestCase):
    def test_add(self):
        self.assertEqual(add(2, 3), 5)
        self.assertEqual(add(-1, 1), 0)

if __name__ == '__main__':
    unittest.main()
```

How it works:

- The add function is tested using the test_add method, which asserts that the sum of 2 + 3 equals 5.
- **unittest.main()** runs the tests when the script is executed.

b. Running Tests Across Multiple Platforms

To run tests on different platforms, you can use **CI/CD pipelines** (like Jenkins or GitHub Actions) to automate the execution of tests on multiple platforms. This ensures that tests are consistently run on Windows, macOS, and Linux.

For example, you can set up a **GitHub Actions** workflow file to run Python tests on multiple platforms:

**Example: GitHub Actions Workflow for Python Testing**

```yaml
yaml

name: Python CI

on: [push]

jobs:
```

```
test:
  runs-on: ${{ matrix.os }}
  strategy:
    matrix:
      os:     [ubuntu-latest,     macos-latest,
windows-latest]
  steps:
    - uses: actions/checkout@v2
    - name: Set up Python
      uses: actions/setup-python@v2
      with:
        python-version: 3.8
    - name: Install dependencies
      run: |
        pip install -r requirements.txt
    - name: Run tests
      run: |
        python -m unittest discover
```

c. UI Testing with Selenium

For **UI testing**, **Selenium** can automate web browsers and ensure that your web-based application works across different environments.

**Example: Using Selenium for Cross-Platform Testing**

```python
python

from selenium import webdriver

# Set up WebDriver for Chrome or Firefox
(depending on the OS)
driver                                    =
webdriver.Chrome(executable_path="/path/to/chro
medriver")

driver.get("http://yourwebsite.com")
```

220

```
assert "Expected Title" in driver.title
```

```
driver.quit()
```

How it works:

- Selenium opens a browser (Chrome in this case), navigates to the webpage, and verifies that the title matches the expected value.
- You can run this test on multiple platforms by using different WebDriver executables or services like **BrowserStack** to run tests on real devices across different browsers.

---

*3. Testing Strategies in C#*

In C#, popular testing frameworks include **xUnit, NUnit,** and **MSTest** for unit testing, and **Appium** or **Selenium** for UI testing. C# integrates well with **Visual Studio** and **Azure DevOps** for running tests on multiple platforms.

a. Unit Testing with xUnit

**xUnit** is one of the most popular testing frameworks in C#, providing support for writing unit tests, assertions, and running tests across different environments.

**Example: Writing Unit Tests with xUnit**

```csharp
using Xunit;

public class MathOperationsTests
```

221

```
{
    [Fact]
    public void TestAdd()
    {
        int result = MathOperations.Add(2, 3);
        Assert.Equal(5, result);
    }
}
```

How it works:

- **[Fact]** defines a test method.
- **Assert.Equal()** checks whether the expected value matches the actual result.

### b. Running Tests Across Multiple Platforms

To ensure that your C# application works across different platforms, you can set up **GitHub Actions**, **Azure Pipelines**, or **Jenkins** for cross-platform testing on Linux, macOS, and Windows.

For **GitHub Actions**:

```yaml
yaml

name: C# CI

on: [push]

jobs:
  build:
    runs-on: ${{ matrix.os }}
    strategy:
      matrix:
        os:    [ubuntu-latest,    macos-latest,
windows-latest]
```

```
steps:
  - uses: actions/checkout@v2
  - name: Set up .NET
    uses: actions/setup-dotnet@v1
    with:
      dotnet-version: '5.0'
  - name: Restore dependencies
    run: dotnet restore
  - name: Build the project
    run: dotnet build
  - name: Run tests
    run: dotnet test
```

c. UI Testing with Appium or Selenium

For **UI testing**, **Appium** or **Selenium** can be used for mobile and web applications, respectively. Both support cross-platform testing, allowing you to write tests that run on Android, iOS, or any web browser.

**Example: UI Testing with Appium for Mobile Apps**

csharp

```
using OpenQA.Selenium.Appium;
using OpenQA.Selenium.Appium.Android;

public class AppiumTests
{
    public void TestAppLaunch()
    {
        AppiumOptions      options      =      new
AppiumOptions();

options.AddAdditionalCapability("platformName",
"Android");
```

```
options.AddAdditionalCapability("deviceName",
"Android Emulator");

        AndroidDriver<AppiumWebElement> driver =
new AndroidDriver<AppiumWebElement>(
        new
Uri("http://127.0.0.1:4723/wd/hub"), options);


driver.FindElementById("com.example:id/button")
.Click();
        Assert.Equal("Expected           Result",
driver.FindElementById("com.example:id/label").
Text);

        driver.Quit();
    }
}
```

How it works:

- **Appium** launches the mobile app on an Android emulator and performs actions (e.g., clicking a button).
- It runs the test on different devices or emulators by adjusting the capabilities.

---

*4. Best Practices for Cross-Platform Testing*

When testing cross-platform applications, it's crucial to ensure consistent behavior across platforms while minimizing platform-specific variations. Here are some best practices for writing cross-platform tests:

224

a. Write Platform-Agnostic Tests

- Focus on writing **unit tests** and **API tests** that do not depend on the platform. For example, writing tests for business logic and backend functionality that runs in the cloud or server-side should be the same regardless of the client's platform.

b. Automate Tests for Multiple Platforms

- Use **CI/CD pipelines** (like GitHub Actions, Jenkins, or Azure Pipelines) to automate the execution of tests across multiple platforms (Windows, macOS, Linux, Android, iOS).
- Set up **cross-platform virtual machines** or use services like **BrowserStack** or **Sauce Labs** to test your application on multiple browsers, devices, and operating systems.

c. Use Emulators and Real Devices

- For mobile apps, it's important to test on **real devices** and not just emulators or simulators. Emulators can help you test common scenarios, but real devices give you a more accurate picture of how your app behaves in the hands of users.

d. Mock Platform-Specific Services

- Use **mocking** to simulate platform-specific services (e.g., location services, device camera) in your tests. Frameworks like **Moq** (C#) or **unittest.mock** (Python) allow you to mock external services during testing.

*5. Conclusion*

Testing cross-platform applications is essential for ensuring consistent and reliable performance across devices and platforms. By using the right testing frameworks and strategies, you can create robust applications that function smoothly regardless of the environment.

In this chapter, we explored:

- Writing **unit tests** and **UI tests** in Python and C#.
- Running cross-platform tests with tools like **GitHub Actions**, **Azure Pipelines**, and **Jenkins**.
- **UI testing** with **Selenium** and **Appium**.
- Best practices for writing and automating cross-platform tests to ensure reliability and consistency.

By adopting these strategies and best practices, you can ensure that your cross-platform apps meet high-quality standards and provide users with a seamless experience across all platforms.

# CHAPTER 24

# CONTINUOUS INTEGRATION/CONTINUOUS DEPLOYMENT (CI/CD)

In modern software development, **Continuous Integration (CI)** and **Continuous Deployment (CD)** are essential practices that help improve the development lifecycle by automating the process of integrating changes and deploying applications. For cross-platform applications, implementing CI/CD pipelines is even more critical, as it ensures consistent building, testing, and deploying of applications across multiple platforms (Windows, macOS, Linux, Android, iOS) from a single codebase.

In this chapter, we will explore how to set up CI/CD pipelines for both **Python** and **C#** cross-platform applications using popular CI/CD tools such as **GitHub Actions**, **Jenkins**, and **GitLab CI**.

---

*1. Introduction to CI/CD for Cross-Platform Applications*

**Continuous Integration (CI)** refers to the practice of frequently integrating code into a shared repository, where automated tests are run to verify the changes.

**Continuous Deployment (CD)** takes CI one step further, automating the release process so that code is automatically deployed to production once it passes the tests.

In cross-platform application development, CI/CD pipelines ensure:

- **Consistency**: The same build and test processes are applied across multiple platforms.
- **Automation**: Builds, tests, and deployments are automated, reducing the manual effort required and the chance of human error.
- **Faster Time to Market**: CI/CD speeds up the release cycle, allowing developers to quickly integrate new features and fixes.

---

*2. Setting Up CI/CD for Python Projects*

For Python projects, we typically use CI/CD tools like **GitHub Actions**, **GitLab CI**, or **Jenkins**. These tools can automate the testing and deployment process for Python-based applications, including web apps, CLI tools, and mobile apps built using frameworks like **Kivy** or **BeeWare**.

a. CI/CD with GitHub Actions for Python

**GitHub Actions** is a powerful CI/CD tool built directly into GitHub. It allows you to define workflows that automate your software development process.

**Example:** `.github/workflows/python-ci.yml` **for Python**

228

```yaml
yaml

name: Python CI/CD

on:
  push:
    branches:
      - main
  pull_request:
    branches:
      - main

jobs:
  build:
    runs-on: ubuntu-latest
    strategy:
      matrix:
        python-version: [3.8, 3.9, 3.10]  # Test on multiple Python versions

    steps:
      - uses: actions/checkout@v2  # Checkout the repository
      - name: Set up Python
        uses: actions/setup-python@v2
        with:
          python-version: ${{ matrix.python-version }}
      - name: Install dependencies
        run: |
          python -m pip install --upgrade pip
          pip install -r requirements.txt
      - name: Run tests
        run: |
          pytest  # Run tests with pytest
      - name: Deploy
        if: success()  # Deploy only if tests pass
```

229

```
run: |
  echo "Deploying the app..."
  # Add your deployment commands here
```

How it works:

1. The workflow is triggered when code is pushed to the `main` branch or a pull request is made.
2. The `build` job runs on **Ubuntu**, but the workflow is set to test multiple Python versions (3.8, 3.9, 3.10).
3. The `steps` section includes:
   - **Checkout** the code.
   - **Set up Python** and install dependencies.
   - Run the tests with **pytest**.
   - Deploy the application if tests pass.

b. CI/CD with GitLab CI for Python

**GitLab CI** is another popular CI/CD tool that integrates well with Python projects.

**Example: `.gitlab-ci.yml` for Python**

yaml

```
stages:
  - install
  - test
  - deploy

install_dependencies:
  stage: install
  image: python:3.9
  script:
    - pip install -r requirements.txt

run_tests:
```

```
  stage: test
  image: python:3.9
  script:
    - pytest

deploy:
  stage: deploy
  script:
    - echo "Deploying the application..."
    - # Add your deployment commands here
  only:
    - main
```

How it works:

- The pipeline has three stages: **install**, **test**, and **deploy**.
- It installs dependencies using `pip`, runs the tests with `pytest`, and deploys the app if tests pass (only on the `main` branch).

c. CI/CD with Jenkins for Python

**Jenkins** is a widely-used automation tool for CI/CD. It allows you to create pipelines for running tests, building, and deploying your Python applications.

**Example: Jenkinsfile for Python**

```groovy

pipeline {
    agent any

    stages {
        stage('Install Dependencies') {
            steps {
```

```
                    sh      'pip      install      -r
requirements.txt'
            }
        }

        stage('Run Tests') {
            steps {
                sh 'pytest'
            }
        }

        stage('Deploy') {
            steps {
                sh 'echo "Deploying the app..."'
                // Add your deployment commands
here
            }
        }
    }
}
```

How it works:

- Jenkins runs the pipeline steps sequentially: installing dependencies, running tests with `pytest`, and deploying if tests pass.

---

*3. Setting Up CI/CD for C# Projects*

For **C# projects**, especially cross-platform mobile applications built using **Xamarin** or **.NET MAUI**, CI/CD pipelines ensure that the code is tested and deployed on multiple platforms (e.g., Android, iOS, Windows).

a. CI/CD with GitHub Actions for C#

**GitHub Actions** can also be used to automate the CI/CD process for C# applications. Below is an example of a simple pipeline for a .NET project.

**Example:** `.github/workflows/dotnet-ci.yml` **for C#**

```yaml
name: .NET Core CI/CD

on:
  push:
    branches:
      - main
  pull_request:
    branches:
      - main

jobs:
  build:
    runs-on: ubuntu-latest
    strategy:
      matrix:
        dotnet-version: ['3.1', '5.0', '6.0']

    steps:
      - uses: actions/checkout@v2
      - name: Set up .NET Core
        uses: actions/setup-dotnet@v1
        with:
          dotnet-version:  ${{  matrix.dotnet-version }}
      - name: Restore dependencies
        run: dotnet restore
      - name: Build
```

233

```
        run:    dotnet    build    --configuration
Release
    - name: Run tests
      run: dotnet test
    - name: Deploy
      if: success()
      run: |
        echo "Deploying the app..."
        # Add your deployment commands here
```

How it works:

- This workflow runs on **Ubuntu** and tests the application on different **.NET versions** (3.1, 5.0, and 6.0).
- It checks out the code, sets up .NET Core, restores dependencies, builds the app, runs tests, and deploys if the tests pass.

b. CI/CD with GitLab CI for C#

**GitLab CI** can be used for automating builds and deployments for .NET projects as well.

**Example: `.gitlab-ci.yml` for C#**

yaml

```
stages:
  - build
  - test
  - deploy

build:
  stage: build
  image: mcr.microsoft.com/dotnet/core/sdk:3.1
  script:
    - dotnet restore
```

234

```
    - dotnet build --configuration Release

test:
  stage: test
  image: mcr.microsoft.com/dotnet/core/sdk:3.1
  script:
    - dotnet test

deploy:
  stage: deploy
  script:
    - echo "Deploying the application..."
    - # Add your deployment commands here
  only:
    - main
```

How it works:

- The pipeline has three stages: **build**, **test**, and **deploy**.
- It builds the .NET application, runs tests, and deploys the app if tests pass.

c. CI/CD with Jenkins for C#

**Jenkins** is commonly used for CI/CD in the .NET ecosystem, especially for Xamarin and .NET MAUI projects.

**Example: Jenkinsfile for C#**

```groovy
groovy

pipeline {
    agent any

    stages {
        stage('Restore') {
```

```
        steps {
            script {
                sh 'dotnet restore'
            }
        }
    }

    stage('Build') {
        steps {
            script {
                sh    'dotnet    build    --
configuration Release'
            }
        }
    }

    stage('Test') {
        steps {
            script {
                sh 'dotnet test'
            }
        }
    }

    stage('Deploy') {
        steps {
            script {
                sh   'echo   "Deploying   the
application..."'
                //   Add   your   deployment
commands here
            }
        }
    }
  }
}
```

How it works:

- **Restore**: The dependencies are restored using `dotnet restore`.
- **Build**: The app is built in Release mode using `dotnet build`.
- **Test**: The tests are run using `dotnet test`.
- **Deploy**: Deploy the app if tests pass.

---

*4. Best Practices for CI/CD in Cross-Platform Development*

To ensure the efficiency and reliability of your CI/CD pipelines for cross-platform applications, consider the following best practices:

a. Automate Testing Across Multiple Platforms

- Ensure that your CI/CD pipeline runs tests on all supported platforms (e.g., Windows, macOS, Android, iOS) to catch platform-specific bugs.

b. Parallelize Jobs

- For faster builds and tests, run jobs in parallel where possible. For example, run **unit tests** on one platform and **UI tests** on another to speed up the testing phase.

c. Use Docker for Consistent Environments

- Use **Docker** to create consistent build environments across different platforms. This ensures that the same environment is used for building and testing on various platforms, reducing inconsistencies.

237

### d. Code Reviews and Automated Tests

- Use **pull request** triggers for your CI/CD pipelines. This ensures that tests are automatically run when changes are made, ensuring that only tested, reviewed code is merged into the main branch.

### e. Continuous Monitoring and Deployment

- Set up monitoring systems to track the health of your deployed applications. Use **Blue-Green Deployment** or **Canary Releases** for safer, gradual rollouts.

---

### 5. Conclusion

In this chapter, we explored how to set up **CI/CD pipelines** for cross-platform applications using **Python** and **C#**. We covered:

- Setting up CI/CD pipelines with **GitHub Actions**, **GitLab CI**, and **Jenkins** for Python and C#.
- Best practices for testing, building, and deploying cross-platform applications.
- Automating the testing process across multiple platforms and devices.

By implementing CI/CD pipelines, you can streamline your development process, reduce errors, and quickly release new features or fixes to users across all platforms.

# CHAPTER 25

# PACKAGING AND DISTRIBUTING CROSS-PLATFORM APPLICATIONS

Once you have developed and tested your cross-platform application, the next crucial step is to package and distribute it so that it reaches your users across multiple platforms (Windows, macOS, Linux, Android, iOS). The process of packaging and distributing an app involves several steps, from preparing the app for distribution to selecting the right platform-specific packaging tools and choosing the appropriate distribution channels.

In this chapter, we will cover the following topics:

1. **Packaging tools** for cross-platform apps.
2. **Distribution strategies** for mobile, desktop, and web platforms.
3. **Best practices** for packaging and distributing cross-platform applications.

---

*1. Packaging Cross-Platform Applications*

The packaging process involves bundling your application into a format that can be installed and executed on different platforms. Depending on the platform, the packaging tools and formats will vary.

### a. Packaging Cross-Platform Desktop Applications

For cross-platform desktop applications, you typically need to package your app as executable files for each platform (e.g., `.exe` for Windows, `.dmg` or `.pkg` for macOS, and `.deb` or `.rpm` for Linux). Here are some common tools:

1. **Electron**: While commonly used with JavaScript, Electron also allows you to use web technologies (HTML, CSS, and JavaScript) to create cross-platform desktop applications. Once the app is ready, you can package it for Windows, macOS, and Linux.
   - **Packaging with Electron**: Electron uses **electron-packager** or **electron-builder** to package and create distributable app files.

   bash

   ```
   # Install electron-packager
   npm install electron-packager --save-dev

   # Package the app
   electron-packager . MyApp --platform=win32
   --arch=x64 --out=dist/
   ```

2. **PyInstaller** (for Python applications): **PyInstaller** is a powerful tool that packages Python applications into stand-alone executables for Windows, macOS, and Linux.
   - **Packaging with PyInstaller**:

```bash
bash

# Install PyInstaller
pip install pyinstaller

# Package the app
pyinstaller --onefile myapp.py
```

3. **.NET MAUI or Xamarin** (for C# applications): For .NET-based applications (e.g., **Xamarin** and **.NET MAUI**), the packaging process is integrated within Visual Studio. These tools allow you to package applications for **Windows** (MSIX), **macOS**, **Linux**, **Android**, and **iOS**.

   o **Packaging with .NET MAUI**: You can use Visual Studio to build and package .NET MAUI apps, or use **MAUI CLI** commands to generate platform-specific packages.

```bash
bash

# Build and package for Android (example)
dotnet    publish    -f:net6.0-android    -c
Release
```

b. Packaging Cross-Platform Mobile Applications

For mobile applications, packaging typically involves creating installation files (e.g., APK for Android and IPA for iOS) that can be installed on devices or submitted to app stores.

1. **Xamarin**:
   o For **Android**, you generate an APK or AAB file (Android App Bundle) for distribution.

- o For **iOS**, you build an IPA file for distribution via the **Apple App Store** or ad-hoc deployment.
- o **Building an APK for Android**:

bash

```
# Build the APK for Android
dotnet build --configuration Release --output ./bin/Release/ --runtime android-arm64
```

- o **Building an IPA for iOS**:

bash

```
# Build the IPA for iOS
dotnet publish -c Release -f:net6.0-ios --output ./bin/iOS/
```

2. **Flutter** (for mobile apps):
   - o **Flutter** supports Android and iOS, and you can use the `flutter build` command to package the app for the respective platforms.
   - o **Building for Android**:

bash

```
flutter build apk
```

- o **Building for iOS**:

bash

```
flutter build ios
```

3. **React Native** (for mobile apps):
   - o **React Native** provides tools to package your mobile app into APK for Android and IPA for iOS.
   - o **Building an APK**:

```bash
npx react-native run-android
```

   - o **Building an IPA**:

```bash
npx react-native run-ios
```

c. Packaging Cross-Platform Web Applications

For web applications, the packaging process typically involves bundling the application into a set of static files (HTML, CSS, JavaScript) and deploying them to a web server.

1. **Vue.js / React / Angular**:
   - o These JavaScript frameworks are used to build cross-platform web applications that can be deployed to various hosting environments.
   - o **Building and bundling the app**:

```bash
# For React
npm run build
```

```
# For Vue.js
npm run build
```

- o The output of the build process is a set of static files (typically located in the `build/` or `dist/` directory).

---

*2. Distribution Strategies for Cross-Platform Applications*

Once your application is packaged, the next step is distribution. The distribution method depends on the platform (desktop, mobile, or web) and the target audience.

a. Distribution of Desktop Applications

1. **Windows (via Microsoft Store)**:
   - o For **Windows**, package your application as an **MSIX** file or an installer (e.g., `.exe` or `.msi`).
   - o You can distribute these files through the **Microsoft Store** or directly via websites.
2. **macOS (via Mac App Store)**:
   - o For **macOS**, package your app as a `.dmg` or `.pkg` file and submit it to the **Mac App Store**.
   - o You can also distribute macOS apps through **third-party websites** or **homebrew**.
3. **Linux**:
   - o For **Linux**, you can create `.deb` or `.rpm` packages for distribution through package managers like **apt** (Debian/Ubuntu) or **yum** (Fedora).
   - o Alternatively, you can distribute as a tarball or AppImage.

b. Distribution of Mobile Applications

1. **Android (via Google Play Store):**
   o For **Android**, you distribute APKs or AABs through the **Google Play Store**.
   o To upload an APK or AAB to the Play Store, use the **Google Play Console**.

2. **iOS (via Apple App Store):**
   o For **iOS**, you package your app as an **IPA** file and distribute it via the **Apple App Store**.
   o You'll need an **Apple Developer account** to submit your app to the App Store.

3. **Ad-Hoc Distribution:**
   o For both Android and iOS, apps can be distributed through **ad-hoc methods** (via email, direct download, or enterprise deployment) for testing or internal use.

c. Distribution of Web Applications

1. **Web Hosting:**
   o For **web apps**, deploy your app to a web server or cloud platform (e.g., **AWS**, **Azure**, **Netlify**, **Vercel**, **Heroku**).
   o Ensure the build artifacts (HTML, CSS, and JavaScript) are correctly deployed to the server.

2. **Progressive Web Apps (PWA):**
   o PWAs allow your web app to act like a native mobile application. You can distribute PWAs directly through a website, or users can install them via the browser.

*3. Best Practices for Packaging and Distributing Cross-Platform Apps*

1. **Automate the Build and Packaging Process**:
   - ○ Use **CI/CD pipelines** to automate the build, test, and deployment process for multiple platforms.
   - ○ Automating the process ensures consistent packaging and reduces human error.

2. **Test on Multiple Platforms**:
   - ○ Before distribution, test your packaged app on all target platforms to ensure it behaves as expected.
   - ○ Use **emulators** and **real devices** to verify the app's functionality across different environments.

3. **Sign and Secure the Application**:
   - ○ Always **sign** your application (e.g., using **code signing certificates**) to ensure its authenticity and prevent tampering during distribution.
   - ○ For **mobile apps**, signing the APK (Android) or IPA (iOS) is mandatory for submitting to app stores.

4. **Optimize the Packaging**:
   - ○ Minimize the size of your packaged app by removing unnecessary files and optimizing assets (images, resources, etc.).
   - ○ For mobile apps, ensure the APK or IPA size is small enough for smooth downloading and installation.

5. **Distribute via Reliable Channels**:
   - ○ Distribute your app through official app stores (Google Play, Apple App Store) for mobile apps to reach the broadest audience.
   - ○ For desktop apps, consider providing multiple installation formats (e.g., `.exe`, `.msi`, `.dmg`, `.pkg`) to support various operating systems.

## 4. Conclusion

Packaging and distributing cross-platform applications is a crucial step in the development process, and it requires selecting the right tools and strategies for each platform. By following the guidelines and best practices outlined in this chapter, you can ensure that your application is packaged correctly and distributed efficiently across different platforms. Whether you're working with desktop, mobile, or web applications, the right packaging tools and distribution channels will help you get your app into users' hands and maintain a smooth user experience across platforms.

# CHAPTER 26

# MANAGING DEPENDENCIES IN CROSS-PLATFORM PROJECTS

One of the challenges in cross-platform development is managing dependencies. Whether you're working with third-party libraries, package managers, or platform-specific dependencies, it's essential to ensure that your application remains stable and compatible across different operating systems (e.g., Windows, macOS, Linux, Android, iOS). In this chapter, we'll explore best practices and tools for managing dependencies in cross-platform projects, ensuring compatibility, and making the process as seamless as possible.

---

*1. Managing Dependencies in Python*

Python provides several tools for managing dependencies, including **pip**, **virtual environments**, and **package managers** like **Poetry** or **Conda**. Managing dependencies in Python allows you to isolate and manage project-specific libraries, ensuring that different projects have their own dependencies without causing conflicts.

a. Using pip and Virtual Environments

**pip** is Python's default package manager and is used to install and manage third-party libraries. When developing cross-platform applications, it's crucial to use **virtual environments** to avoid conflicts between libraries required by different projects.

1. **Creating a Virtual Environment:** A **virtual environment** is a self-contained directory that contains all the dependencies for a Python project.

   bash

   ```
   python3 -m venv myenv  # Create a virtual
   environment
   source myenv/bin/activate  # Activate the
   virtual environment (Linux/macOS)
   myenv\Scripts\activate    # Activate  the
   virtual environment (Windows)
   ```

2. **Installing Dependencies with pip:** Use `pip` to install dependencies into the virtual environment.

   bash

   ```
   pip install requests  # Install a library
   ```

3. **Managing Dependencies with requirements.txt:** For project portability, save all the dependencies in a `requirements.txt` file.

   bash

```
pip  freeze  >  requirements.txt    #  Save
installed dependencies
```

To install the dependencies listed in the file:

```
bash
```

```
pip install -r requirements.txt
```

b. Using Poetry for Dependency Management

**Poetry** is a Python dependency management tool that handles packaging, dependencies, and virtual environments all in one. It simplifies the process of adding, updating, and managing dependencies.

1. **Install Poetry:**

   ```
   bash
   ```

   ```
   pip install poetry
   ```

2. **Creating a New Project with Poetry:**

   ```
   bash
   ```

   ```
   poetry new myproject
   ```

3. **Adding Dependencies:**

   ```
   bash
   ```

   ```
   poetry add requests
   ```

4. **Installing Dependencies:**

```bash
poetry install
```

Poetry helps maintain consistent dependency versions across platforms, and it also generates a `pyproject.toml` file, which contains detailed information about the project's dependencies.

c. Using Conda for Cross-Platform Dependency Management

**Conda** is a package manager that works across platforms, including Python and non-Python dependencies. It is widely used in data science but can be useful for any project that requires managing complex dependencies.

1. **Create a Conda Environment:**

```bash
conda create --name myenv python=3.9
```

2. **Activate the Environment:**

```bash
conda activate myenv
```

3. **Install Dependencies:**

```bash
conda install requests
```

4. **Exporting Environment:**

251

```bash
conda list --export > environment.txt
```

To recreate the environment on a different machine:

```bash
conda    create    --name    myenv    --file
environment.txt
```

d. Handling Platform-Specific Dependencies in Python

Some Python libraries might have platform-specific dependencies or require additional setup on specific platforms (e.g., `pyobjc` for macOS or `pywin32` for Windows).

- Use **conditional imports** and package installation based on the platform to handle platform-specific dependencies.

```python
import sys

if sys.platform == "win32":
    import win32com.client
elif sys.platform == "darwin":
    import objc
```

You can also use `platform` or `sys` modules to check the operating system before installing certain dependencies.

*2. Managing Dependencies in C#*

In C#, managing dependencies is primarily done using **NuGet**, the package manager for the .NET ecosystem. **.NET Core** and **.NET MAUI** applications use **NuGet packages** for managing third-party libraries and project dependencies.

a. Using NuGet for Dependency Management

1. **Adding a NuGet Package:**
   - You can add a NuGet package to a C# project using the **dotnet CLI** or **Visual Studio**.

   bash

   ```
   dotnet add package Newtonsoft.Json
   ```

2. **Restoring Dependencies:**
   - After cloning a repository or pulling changes, use the following command to restore dependencies:

   bash

   ```
   dotnet restore
   ```

3. **Listing Installed NuGet Packages:**
   - To see the installed packages, you can use:

   bash

   ```
   dotnet list package
   ```

b. Managing Cross-Platform Dependencies with .NET SDK

With **.NET Core** and **.NET MAUI**, dependencies are specified in the `.csproj` file. This file can include dependencies that target different platforms.

**Example: `.csproj` File for Cross-Platform App**

xml

```
<Project Sdk="Microsoft.NET.Sdk">

  <PropertyGroup>
    <TargetFramework>net6.0</TargetFramework>
    <UseWPF>false</UseWPF>
    <UseWindowsForms>false</UseWindowsForms>
  </PropertyGroup>

  <ItemGroup>
    <PackageReference   Include="Newtonsoft.Json"
Version="13.0.1" />
    <PackageReference
Include="Xamarin.Essentials" Version="1.7.0" />
  </ItemGroup>

</Project>
```

This ensures that when the project is built for different platforms, the correct dependencies are included.

c. Managing Platform-Specific Dependencies in C#

For managing platform-specific dependencies in C#, you can use conditional compilation or multi-targeting to target specific platforms.

1. **Using Multi-Targeting:**
   o You can target multiple platforms by specifying target frameworks in the `.csproj` file.

xml

```xml
<TargetFrameworks>net6.0-android;net6.0-
ios;net6.0-windows</TargetFrameworks>
```

2. **Platform-Specific Code with Conditional Compilation:**

csharp

```csharp
#if WINDOWS
    // Windows-specific code
#elif ANDROID
    // Android-specific code
#elif IOS
    // iOS-specific code
#endif
```

This helps to isolate platform-specific dependencies and code, ensuring that the application behaves properly on each platform.

---

### 3. Ensuring Compatibility Across Platforms

Ensuring compatibility across multiple platforms requires more than just managing dependencies—it requires thoughtful design choices and the right tools to handle platform-specific scenarios.

## a. Use Cross-Platform Libraries

For cross-platform applications, choose libraries and frameworks that support all your target platforms. For example:

- **Xamarin** and **.NET MAUI** for C# apps.
- **Kivy**, **BeeWare**, or **PyQt** for Python apps.

## b. Test on Multiple Platforms

Use **CI/CD** pipelines (like **GitHub Actions**, **GitLab CI**, or **Jenkins**) to run automated tests across all your target platforms. Ensure that:

- Your application works on different operating systems (e.g., Windows, macOS, Linux).
- Your app runs on different device types (e.g., desktop, tablet, smartphone).

## c. Use Cross-Platform Tools and Abstractions

Leverage platform abstraction libraries to simplify platform-specific logic. For example:

- In C#, **Xamarin.Essentials** provides APIs for device features (camera, geolocation, sensors) that work across Android and iOS.
- In Python, **Kivy** or **PyQt** provides abstractions for UI and device features that work on multiple platforms.

### d. Handle Platform-Specific APIs Carefully

For platforms where a particular library doesn't work universally (e.g., iOS-only or Android-only libraries), use **dependency injection** or platform-specific code (via `sys.platform` in Python or `#if` directives in C#) to manage these dependencies appropriately.

---

### 4. Conclusion

Managing dependencies in cross-platform projects requires a structured approach to ensure compatibility and maintainability. By leveraging the right tools—such as **virtual environments** and **Poetry** in Python, or **NuGet** and **multi-targeting** in C#—and adopting best practices for managing platform-specific dependencies, you can create applications that are easy to maintain, scalable, and compatible across multiple platforms.

In this chapter, we covered:

- Managing dependencies in **Python** with tools like **pip**, **Poetry**, and **Conda**.
- Managing dependencies in **C#** with **NuGet** and **.NET SDK**.
- Ensuring compatibility across multiple platforms using **cross-platform libraries**, **CI/CD pipelines**, and **platform-specific code**.

By following these strategies and tools, you can simplify the dependency management process and focus on building cross-platform applications that are reliable and efficient.

# CHAPTER 27

# CASE STUDY 1: CROSS-PLATFORM DESKTOP APPLICATION

In this case study, we will explore the development of a **cross-platform desktop application** using both **Python** and **C#**. The goal is to compare the development process in each language, highlighting the advantages and challenges of building cross-platform desktop apps. The application we'll build is a simple **task manager**, where users can manage tasks, mark them as completed, and filter tasks based on their status. The application will be designed to run on **Windows**, **macOS**, and **Linux**.

By the end of this chapter, you will have a comprehensive understanding of how to create cross-platform desktop applications using Python and C#, and how the development processes differ between the two languages.

---

*1. Overview of the Cross-Platform Task Manager Application*

The task manager application we'll develop will have the following features:

- A **list of tasks**, each with a title, description, and completion status.
- Options to **add**, **edit**, or **delete** tasks.
- A **filter** option to view tasks by their completion status (e.g., completed or pending).
- A **simple user interface** that works seamlessly across multiple platforms.

Platforms Targeted:

- **Windows**
- **macOS**
- **Linux**

Frameworks/Tools Used:

- **Python**: We'll use **Tkinter** (for UI) and **SQLite** (for the database).
- **C#**: We'll use **.NET MAUI** (for cross-platform UI) and **SQLite** (for the database).

---

*2. Building the Cross-Platform Task Manager in Python*

Python offers several frameworks for building cross-platform desktop applications, but we will use **Tkinter**, which is the standard GUI library for Python, and **SQLite** for storing tasks locally.

a. Setting Up the Python Project

1. **Install the Required Libraries**:
   - ○ **Tkinter** is included with Python by default, so no installation is required.

      o **SQLite** support is built into Python as well (via the `sqlite3` module).

2. **Create the Main Application File (`task_manager.py`):**

Here's a simplified example of how the task manager application can be structured using **Tkinter** and **SQLite**:

```python
python

import tkinter as tk
from tkinter import messagebox
import sqlite3

# Database setup
conn = sqlite3.connect('tasks.db')
c = conn.cursor()
c.execute('''CREATE TABLE IF NOT EXISTS tasks (id
INTEGER PRIMARY KEY, title TEXT, description
TEXT, completed BOOLEAN)''')
conn.commit()

# Functions to interact with the database
def add_task(title, description):
    c.execute("INSERT    INTO    tasks    (title,
description, completed) VALUES (?, ?, ?)",
(title, description, False))
    conn.commit()

def get_tasks():
    c.execute("SELECT * FROM tasks")
    return c.fetchall()

def update_task(task_id, completed):
    c.execute("UPDATE tasks SET completed = ?
WHERE id = ?", (completed, task_id))
    conn.commit()
```

```python
def delete_task(task_id):
    c.execute("DELETE FROM tasks WHERE id = ?",
(task_id,))
    conn.commit()

# GUI Setup
class TaskManagerApp:
    def __init__(self, root):
        self.root = root
        self.root.title("Task Manager")

        # Task Listbox
        self.task_listbox                    =
tk.Listbox(self.root, width=50, height=10)
        self.task_listbox.grid(row=0, column=0,
columnspan=3)

        # Add Task Button
        self.add_button  =  tk.Button(self.root,
text="Add Task", command=self.add_task)
        self.add_button.grid(row=1, column=0)

        # Delete Task Button
        self.delete_button                   =
tk.Button(self.root,    text="Delete    Task",
command=self.delete_task)
        self.delete_button.grid(row=1, column=1)

        # Update Task Button
        self.update_button                   =
tk.Button(self.root,   text="Complete    Task",
command=self.update_task)
        self.update_button.grid(row=1, column=2)

        # Load and display tasks
        self.load_tasks()
```

```python
    def load_tasks(self):
        tasks = get_tasks()
        self.task_listbox.delete(0, tk.END)
        for task in tasks:
            status = "Completed" if task[3] else
"Pending"
            self.task_listbox.insert(tk.END,
f"{task[1]} - {status}")

    def add_task(self):
        title = "New Task"
        description = "Task Description"
        add_task(title, description)
        self.load_tasks()

    def delete_task(self):
        selected_task                          =
self.task_listbox.curselection()
        if selected_task:
            task_id                            =
get_tasks()[selected_task[0]][0]
            delete_task(task_id)
            self.load_tasks()

    def update_task(self):
        selected_task                          =
self.task_listbox.curselection()
        if selected_task:
            task_id                            =
get_tasks()[selected_task[0]][0]
            current_status                     =
get_tasks()[selected_task[0]][3]
            new_status = not current_status
            update_task(task_id, new_status)
            self.load_tasks()

# Run the app
if __name__ == "__main__":
```

```
root = tk.Tk()
app = TaskManagerApp(root)
root.mainloop()
```

How it works:

- **SQLite Database**: The application uses an SQLite database to store tasks with `id`, `title`, `description`, and `completed` fields.
- **Tkinter UI**: The GUI allows users to interact with tasks by adding, updating, or deleting them.
- The `load_tasks()` method populates the task list with tasks from the database.
- The app supports basic CRUD operations (Create, Read, Update, Delete).

Running the App:

- This Python app can be run on **Windows**, **macOS**, and **Linux** without modification, thanks to Tkinter's cross-platform compatibility.

---

*3. Building the Cross-Platform Task Manager in C#*

For C#, we'll use **.NET MAUI**, which is a cross-platform framework for building applications that run on Android, iOS, macOS, and Windows with a single codebase. In this case study, we'll develop the same task manager app using **.NET MAUI** and **SQLite**.

a. Setting Up the C# Project

1. **Install Visual Studio with .NET MAUI:**

- o Install Visual Studio with the **Mobile development with .NET** and **.NET MAUI** workloads to create cross-platform apps.
2. **Create a New .NET MAUI Project**:
   - o Create a new **.NET MAUI** project using Visual Studio.
3. **Add SQLite NuGet Package**:
   - o Use **SQLite-net-pcl** to interact with the SQLite database in .NET MAUI.

```bash
dotnet add package SQLite-net-pcl
```

b. Creating the Task Manager App with .NET MAUI

Here's an example of how the C# application can be structured using **.NET MAUI** for the task manager:

```csharp
using SQLite;
using Microsoft.Maui.Controls;

public class Task
{
    [PrimaryKey, AutoIncrement]
    public int Id { get; set; }
    public string Title { get; set; }
    public string Description { get; set; }
    public bool Completed { get; set; }
}

public class MainPage : ContentPage
{
    private SQLiteConnection _database;
    private ListView _taskListView;
```

```
public MainPage()
{
    _database                =            new
SQLiteConnection("tasks.db");
    _database.CreateTable<Task>();

    _taskListView = new ListView();
    _taskListView.ItemTemplate    =     new
DataTemplate(() =>
    {
        var textCell = new TextCell();

textCell.SetBinding(TextCell.TextProperty,
"Title");

textCell.SetBinding(TextCell.DetailProperty,
"Completed");
        return textCell;
    });

    var addButton = new Button { Text = "Add
Task" };
    addButton.Clicked += OnAddTaskClicked;

    var completeButton = new Button { Text =
"Complete Task" };
    completeButton.Clicked               +=
OnCompleteTaskClicked;

    var deleteButton = new Button { Text =
"Delete Task" };
    deleteButton.Clicked                 +=
OnDeleteTaskClicked;

    var stackLayout = new StackLayout
    {
```

```
        Children    =    {    _taskListView,
addButton, completeButton, deleteButton }
    };

    Content = stackLayout;

    LoadTasks();
}

private void LoadTasks()
{
    var            tasks            =
_database.Table<Task>().ToList();
    _taskListView.ItemsSource = tasks;
}

private void OnAddTaskClicked(object sender,
EventArgs e)
{
    var task = new Task { Title = "New Task",
Description = "Task Description", Completed =
false };
    _database.Insert(task);
    LoadTasks();
}

private void OnCompleteTaskClicked(object
sender, EventArgs e)
{
    if (_taskListView.SelectedItem is Task
selectedTask)
    {
        selectedTask.Completed            =
!selectedTask.Completed;
        _database.Update(selectedTask);
        LoadTasks();
    }
}
```

```
    private    void    OnDeleteTaskClicked(object
sender, EventArgs e)
    {
        if (_taskListView.SelectedItem is Task
selectedTask)
        {
            _database.Delete(selectedTask);
            LoadTasks();
        }
    }
}
```

How it works:

- **SQLite Database**: The application uses an SQLite database to store tasks.
- **.NET MAUI UI**: The app's UI consists of a `ListView` to display tasks and buttons for adding, completing, or deleting tasks.
- The `LoadTasks()` method populates the task list with tasks from the SQLite database.

Running the App:

- This C# app can be run on **Windows, macOS, Android**, and **iOS** without modification, thanks to .NET MAUI's cross-platform support.

---

*4. Key Differences and Considerations*

While both Python and C# offer solid frameworks for building cross-platform applications, there are key differences in how the development and packaging processes work:

| Feature | Python (Tkinter) | C# (.NET MAUI) |
|---|---|---|
| UI Framework | Tkinter | .NET MAUI |
| Packaging Tools | PyInstaller, cx_Freeze | Visual Studio (MSIX, APK, IPA) |
| Database | SQLite (via sqlite3 module) | SQLite (via `SQLite-net-pcl`) |
| Cross-Platform Support | Windows, macOS, Linux | Windows, macOS, Android, iOS |
| Deployment | Manual packaging or setup tools | Integrated with Visual Studio (App Stores) |
| Development Speed | Faster setup for small projects | Requires more setup, but more robust |

## 5. Conclusion

In this case study, we have explored how to build a **cross-platform task manager application** using both **Python** (with Tkinter and SQLite) and **C#** (with .NET MAUI and SQLite). While both approaches offer a way to develop cross-platform apps, the choice between Python and C# depends on factors like development speed, platform requirements, and long-term scalability.

- **Python** with **Tkinter** provides a simple and fast solution for building desktop apps on multiple platforms but may lack the native look and feel.

269

- **C# with .NET MAUI** provides a more comprehensive, native approach to building cross-platform applications, especially for mobile and desktop, though it may require more setup.

By following the examples provided, you can apply similar principles to develop more complex cross-platform applications in both languages.

# CHAPTER 28

# CASE STUDY 2: CROSS-PLATFORM MOBILE APPLICATION

In this case study, we will walk through the process of building a **cross-platform mobile application** using both **C#** and **Python**. The goal of this chapter is to compare the two approaches and show the different tools and frameworks used in both ecosystems to create cross-platform mobile apps.

We'll build a simple **To-Do List app** that allows users to:

1. Add, view, and delete tasks.
2. Mark tasks as completed.
3. Display a list of tasks on a mobile interface.

By the end of this chapter, you will have a clear understanding of how to build mobile apps using both **C#** (with **Xamarin** or **.NET MAUI**) and **Python** (with **Kivy** or **BeeWare**), and understand the strengths and challenges of each approach.

*1. Overview of the Cross-Platform Mobile App*

The mobile application we'll build will have the following features:

- A **list of tasks**, with options to add, delete, and mark tasks as completed.
- A **simple user interface** for interacting with the tasks.
- The app will be designed to run on **Android** and **iOS** using cross-platform frameworks.

Platforms Targeted:

- **Android**
- **iOS**

Frameworks/Tools Used:

- **Python**: We will use **Kivy** (for UI) and **SQLite** (for local storage).
- **C#**: We will use **Xamarin** or **.NET MAUI** (for UI) and **SQLite** (for local storage).

---

*2. Building the Cross-Platform Mobile App in Python (Using Kivy)*

**Kivy** is a Python library for developing multitouch applications. It is well-suited for building mobile applications that run on both **Android** and **iOS**.

a. Setting Up the Python Project with Kivy

1. **Install Kivy and Dependencies:**

```bash
bash
```

```bash
pip install kivy
pip install kivy-examples  # Optional: for
exploring Kivy examples
```

## 2. Create the Project (todo_app.py):

Here is a simplified version of the To-Do List application using **Kivy** and **SQLite**:

```python
python

import kivy
from kivy.app import App
from kivy.uix.button import Button
from kivy.uix.boxlayout import BoxLayout
from kivy.uix.textinput import TextInput
from kivy.uix.label import Label
from kivy.uix.scrollview import ScrollView
from kivy.uix.checkbox import CheckBox
import sqlite3

# Create or open SQLite database
conn = sqlite3.connect('tasks.db')
c = conn.cursor()
c.execute('''CREATE TABLE IF NOT EXISTS tasks (id
INTEGER PRIMARY KEY, title TEXT, completed
BOOLEAN)''')
conn.commit()

# Functions to interact with database
def add_task(title):
    c.execute("INSERT INTO tasks (title,
completed) VALUES (?, ?)", (title, False))
    conn.commit()
```

273

```python
def get_tasks():
    c.execute("SELECT * FROM tasks")
    return c.fetchall()

def delete_task(task_id):
    c.execute("DELETE FROM tasks WHERE id = ?",
(task_id,))
    conn.commit()

def update_task(task_id, completed):
    c.execute("UPDATE tasks SET completed = ?
WHERE id = ?", (completed, task_id))
    conn.commit()

class ToDoApp(App):
    def build(self):
        self.root                              =
BoxLayout(orientation='vertical')
        self.scroll_view = ScrollView()
        self.task_layout                       =
BoxLayout(orientation='vertical',
size_hint_y=None)

self.task_layout.bind(minimum_height=self.task_
layout.setter('height'))

self.scroll_view.add_widget(self.task_layout)

        self.input_task                        =
TextInput(hint_text='Enter            task...',
size_hint_y=None, height=40)
        self.add_button     =     Button(text='Add
Task', size_hint_y=None, height=40)

self.add_button.bind(on_press=self.add_task)

        self.root.add_widget(self.input_task)
        self.root.add_widget(self.add_button)
```

274

```
        self.root.add_widget(self.scroll_view)

        self.load_tasks()
        return self.root

    def load_tasks(self):
        self.task_layout.clear_widgets()
        tasks = get_tasks()
        for task in tasks:
            task_button                        =
BoxLayout(size_hint_y=None, height=40)
            label         =        Label(text=task[1],
size_hint_x=0.8)
            checkbox = CheckBox(active=task[2],
size_hint_x=0.2)
            checkbox.bind(active=lambda
checkbox,                  task_id=task[0]:
self.toggle_task(checkbox, task_id))
            delete_button                      =
Button(text='Delete', size_hint_x=0.2)
            delete_button.bind(on_press=lambda
btn, task_id=task[0]: self.delete_task(task_id))
            task_button.add_widget(label)
            task_button.add_widget(checkbox)

task_button.add_widget(delete_button)

self.task_layout.add_widget(task_button)

    def add_task(self, instance):
        title = self.input_task.text
        if title:
            add_task(title)
            self.input_task.text = ''
            self.load_tasks()

    def delete_task(self, task_id):
        delete_task(task_id)
```

275

```
            self.load_tasks()

    def toggle_task(self, checkbox, task_id):
        update_task(task_id, checkbox.active)
        self.load_tasks()

if __name__ == '__main__':
    ToDoApp().run()
```

How it works:

- The application uses **SQLite** to store the tasks locally.
- **Kivy UI**: The user interface consists of a text input for adding tasks, a scrollable list of tasks, and buttons for deleting or marking tasks as complete.
- The application supports both **Android** and **iOS**, and it runs seamlessly on both platforms when packaged using **Buildozer** for Android or **Xcode** for iOS.

Running the App:

1. For Android, you can package the app using **Buildozer**.

```bash
bash

buildozer android debug
```

2. For iOS, you can use **Xcode** to package and run the app on a device or simulator.

*3. Building the Cross-Platform Mobile App in C# (Using .NET MAUI)*

For **C#**, we will use **.NET MAUI**, which is a modern cross-platform framework for building mobile and desktop applications. .NET MAUI allows you to write a single codebase that runs on Android, iOS, macOS, and Windows.

a. Setting Up the C# Project with .NET MAUI

1. **Install .NET MAUI:**
   o Install Visual Studio 2022 with the **.NET MAUI** workload.
   o Create a new **.NET MAUI** project from the **New Project** wizard in Visual Studio.
2. **Create the Project (TodoApp.cs):**

Here is the equivalent To-Do List application in **C#** using **.NET MAUI** and **SQLite**:

```csharp
csharp

using SQLite;
using Microsoft.Maui.Controls;
using System.Collections.ObjectModel;

public class Task
{
    [PrimaryKey, AutoIncrement]
    public int Id { get; set; }
    public string Title { get; set; }
    public bool Completed { get; set; }
}

public partial class MainPage : ContentPage
{
```

```
private SQLiteConnection _database;
private ObservableCollection<Task> _tasks;

public MainPage()
{
    InitializeComponent();
    _database                =                new
SQLiteConnection("tasks.db");
    _database.CreateTable<Task>();

    _tasks                  =                new
ObservableCollection<Task>(_database.Table<Task
>().ToList());
    taskListView.ItemsSource = _tasks;
}

private    void    AddTask(object    sender,
EventArgs e)
{
    var    task   =   new   Task   {   Title   =
taskEntry.Text, Completed = false };
    _database.Insert(task);
    _tasks.Add(task);
    taskEntry.Text = string.Empty;
}

private    void    DeleteTask(object    sender,
EventArgs e)
{
    if  (taskListView.SelectedItem  is  Task
selectedTask)
    {
        _database.Delete(selectedTask);
        _tasks.Remove(selectedTask);
    }
}
```

```
    private    void    ToggleTask(object    sender,
EventArgs e)
    {
        if  (taskListView.SelectedItem  is  Task
selectedTask)
        {
            selectedTask.Completed              =
!selectedTask.Completed;
            _database.Update(selectedTask);
            taskListView.ItemsSource    =    new
ObservableCollection<Task>(_database.Table<Task
>().ToList());
        }
    }
}
```

How it works:

- The app uses **SQLite** for data storage.
- **.NET MAUI UI**: The interface includes a text input for adding tasks, a list view for displaying tasks, and buttons for adding, deleting, or marking tasks as complete.
- The application can be deployed to **Android** and **iOS** with **Visual Studio**'s built-in tools.

Running the App:

1. **Android**: Use **Visual Studio** to build and deploy the app to an Android emulator or real device.
2. **iOS**: You can use **Xcode** for iOS deployment if you're on macOS.

279

*4. Key Differences and Considerations*

| Feature | Python (Kivy) | C# (.NET MAUI) |
| --- | --- | --- |
| UI Framework | Kivy | .NET MAUI |
| Package Management | pip, setuptools, Buildozer | NuGet, MSBuild, Visual Studio |
| Database | SQLite via `sqlite3` module | SQLite via `SQLite-net-pcl` |
| Cross-Platform Support | Android, iOS, Windows, Linux | Android, iOS, macOS, Windows |
| Performance | Suitable for simple apps | Native performance with optimization |
| Development Speed | Faster for prototyping and small apps | More robust, especially for mobile apps |
| Deployment Tools | Buildozer for Android, Xcode for iOS | Visual Studio, MSIX, APK, IPA |

- **Python (Kivy)** is great for rapidly developing simple apps and prototypes. It works well for apps that don't require complex platform-specific UI or performance optimizations.
- **C# (.NET MAUI)** provides more robust tools for building production-grade applications with native UI components and better integration with mobile operating systems like Android and iOS.

280

*5. Conclusion*

In this case study, we built a **cross-platform mobile app** using both **Python (Kivy)** and **C# (.NET MAUI)**. We learned:

- How to set up a simple mobile app with task management functionality.
- How to store tasks in a local SQLite database in both Python and C#.
- The differences in tools, frameworks, and deployment strategies between Python and C#.

Both Python and C# offer strong frameworks for building cross-platform mobile applications, and the choice between them depends on your specific needs:

- **Python (Kivy)** is more suited for simpler, smaller-scale applications and rapid prototyping.
- **C# (.NET MAUI)** is more suited for production-quality mobile applications that require high performance and deep integration with platform-specific features.

4o mini

You said:

25. Future Trends in Cross-Platform Development Discussion on the future of cross-platform development, emerging technologies, and how Python and C# are evolving to meet new challenges.

# CHAPTER 29

# FUTURE TRENDS IN CROSS-PLATFORM DEVELOPMENT

Cross-platform development has seen significant evolution in recent years, with frameworks like **Xamarin**, **Flutter**, **React Native**, and **.NET MAUI** gaining widespread adoption. The demand for applications that run seamlessly across multiple platforms, including **mobile**, **desktop**, and **web**, continues to grow. In this chapter, we will discuss the future of cross-platform development, explore emerging technologies, and look at how **Python** and **C#** are evolving to meet new challenges.

*1. The Growing Need for Cross-Platform Development*

As businesses and developers aim to target broader user bases, the demand for cross-platform development is increasing. This is driven by several factors:

- **Multiple Devices and Platforms**: Users expect applications to work seamlessly across a wide variety of platforms, including smartphones, tablets, desktops, and the web.
- **Cost Efficiency**: Developing separate apps for each platform is time-consuming and costly. Cross-platform

development allows developers to maintain a single codebase while delivering apps for multiple platforms.

- **Unified User Experiences**: Cross-platform development frameworks enable developers to offer a consistent user experience, ensuring that applications look and feel the same across different platforms.

## 2. Emerging Trends in Cross-Platform Development

Several emerging technologies and trends are shaping the future of cross-platform development:

### a. The Rise of WebAssembly (Wasm)

**WebAssembly** (Wasm) is a binary instruction format that allows high-performance execution of code in web browsers. It enables developers to compile languages like C, C++, Rust, and even Python into bytecode that runs in browsers at near-native speeds.

- **Cross-Platform Potential**: WebAssembly is becoming a game-changer for building cross-platform applications, as it allows code to run natively in web browsers, providing a way to build lightweight, fast, and cross-platform web apps.
- **Impact on Python and C#**: Both Python and C# have seen progress in compiling their code to WebAssembly, allowing developers to run Python or C# applications directly in browsers without relying on traditional JavaScript-based solutions.

**Example**:

- **Python**: **Pyodide** is a Python distribution that compiles Python to WebAssembly, making it possible to run Python code in the browser.
- **C#**: **Blazor WebAssembly** allows developers to write C# code that runs in the browser through WebAssembly, enabling seamless client-side development with .NET technologies.

### b. Advancements in Mobile Development Frameworks

Cross-platform mobile development is one of the most actively evolving areas, with frameworks like **Flutter**, **React Native**, and **.NET MAUI** pushing the boundaries of what is possible for mobile applications.

- **Flutter**: **Flutter**, developed by Google, is gaining popularity for building high-performance, visually rich mobile apps with a single codebase for Android, iOS, and the web. Flutter allows developers to write apps in **Dart**, a language designed for client-side development, and provides a reactive framework for building UIs.
- **React Native**: React Native continues to evolve as one of the leading frameworks for building cross-platform mobile apps using **JavaScript** and **React**. React Native has made significant strides in improving performance and access to native APIs, making it a popular choice for mobile app development.
- **.NET MAUI**: .NET MAUI (Multi-platform App UI) is Microsoft's evolution of Xamarin, allowing developers to write cross-platform apps for Android,

284

iOS, macOS, and Windows. .NET MAUI simplifies UI development by using a single codebase and supports native performance across all platforms.

- **Impact on C#**: **.NET MAUI** and **Xamarin** are at the forefront of cross-platform mobile development in the C# ecosystem. .NET MAUI is expected to further unify mobile and desktop development under a single framework, making it easier for developers to build apps across all devices.

c. Progressive Web Apps (PWAs) and Cross-Platform Web Development

**Progressive Web Apps (PWAs)** are web applications that behave like native mobile apps. PWAs can be installed on a device and accessed offline, while still leveraging the benefits of web technologies (HTML, CSS, JavaScript).

- **Cross-Platform Potential**: PWAs are inherently cross-platform since they run in the web browser, making them a great solution for building apps that work across mobile, tablet, and desktop environments.
- **Advantages**: PWAs combine the best of both worlds—web apps and mobile apps—offering native-like functionality with the ease of web deployment. They also reduce the complexity of developing native mobile apps for multiple platforms.

**Impact on Python and C#**:

- **Python**: Python frameworks like **Flask** and **Django** can be used to build web applications, while **Pyodide** and

**Brython** allow Python to run in the browser as part of PWAs.

- **C#**: With **Blazor** (part of the .NET ecosystem), developers can build **SPA** (Single Page Applications) and PWAs using C#. This allows the development of cross-platform web apps with C# that run on any browser without the need for JavaScript.

### d. Cloud-Native and Serverless Architectures

Cloud-native and **serverless architectures** are becoming increasingly popular for cross-platform applications. Serverless computing allows developers to focus on writing code without managing the underlying infrastructure, and cloud-native applications are designed to run on cloud platforms, making them inherently cross-platform.

- **Serverless**: Technologies like **AWS Lambda**, **Azure Functions**, and **Google Cloud Functions** enable serverless computing, allowing backend logic to run on-demand without managing servers. This reduces complexity and ensures your app scales seamlessly across platforms.
- **Cloud-Native**: Cloud-native apps are built to fully leverage cloud infrastructure and services, ensuring high availability and cross-platform compatibility.

**Impact on Python and C#:**

- **Python**: Python is widely supported by serverless platforms, with frameworks like **Zappa** and **Serverless Framework** simplifying the deployment of Python applications to serverless environments.

286

- **C#**: C# and **.NET Core** are also well-suited for serverless computing, with Azure Functions and AWS Lambda supporting C# for serverless application development.

---

*3. How Python and C# Are Evolving for Cross-Platform Development*

As the demand for cross-platform applications grows, both **Python** and **C#** are evolving to meet new challenges and provide better support for building cross-platform apps.

a. Python's Evolution in Cross-Platform Development

Python has traditionally been used for backend development, scripting, and automation, but it has steadily gained traction for cross-platform app development.

1. **WebAssembly (Wasm)**: Python is increasingly being compiled to **WebAssembly**, enabling Python code to run in browsers. Tools like **Pyodide** and **PyScript** are making Python a viable option for web-based applications.
2. **Mobile Development**: Although Python is not typically used for mobile development, tools like **BeeWare** and **Kivy** are slowly gaining popularity for building mobile apps. **BeeWare** provides a Python interface for building native UIs, while **Kivy** offers tools for building graphical applications that run across platforms.
3. **Data Science and AI**: Python's role in **data science** and **AI** continues to grow, and its integration with cross-platform tools ensures that Python remains relevant for building cross-platform applications that involve data processing, machine learning, and AI.

### b. C#'s Evolution in Cross-Platform Development

C# and the **.NET ecosystem** have undergone major improvements in recent years, making C# a top choice for building cross-platform applications.

1. **.NET MAUI**: .NET MAUI is the successor to Xamarin and is part of the **.NET 6/7** framework. It allows developers to build cross-platform mobile and desktop apps with a single codebase, targeting Android, iOS, macOS, and Windows.
2. **Blazor**: **Blazor** allows C# developers to build web applications with **WebAssembly**. By using Blazor, C# code can run directly in the browser, making it a powerful tool for building **cross-platform web apps**.
3. **Cloud and Serverless**: C#'s integration with **Azure** and **AWS** makes it an excellent choice for building cloud-native and serverless applications, further strengthening its place in the cross-platform ecosystem.

---

### 4. Future Challenges and Opportunities

While the future of cross-platform development is promising, there are still challenges to address:

- **Performance Optimization**: Ensuring native-like performance across all platforms is a constant challenge. Frameworks like **Flutter** and **.NET MAUI** are working to bridge this gap, but performance can still vary across devices.
- **Platform-Specific Features**: While cross-platform frameworks provide abstraction layers, accessing advanced platform-specific features (e.g., advanced

camera APIs, system-level integrations) may still require native code.

- **User Experience Consistency**: Ensuring that your app provides a native-like experience on all platforms remains a key challenge. Frameworks are improving in this regard, but developers still need to be mindful of UI guidelines and performance nuances for each platform.

However, with the ongoing evolution of frameworks like **.NET MAUI**, **Flutter**, **React Native**, and the rise of **WebAssembly**, the future of cross-platform development looks bright, and both **Python** and **C#** are well-positioned to take advantage of these emerging trends.

---

## 5. Conclusion

Cross-platform development has become more important than ever as the demand for apps that work across multiple devices and operating systems continues to rise. The evolution of **Python** and **C#** to address these challenges has led to powerful frameworks like **.NET MAUI, Xamarin, Flutter**, and **Kivy**, which allow developers to build apps that run on **mobile, desktop**, and **web** platforms with a single codebase.

As **WebAssembly** and **serverless architectures** gain traction, both Python and C# are adapting to meet the needs of modern cross-platform development. The future will see even more seamless integrations between different platforms, more advanced cloud capabilities, and further advancements in native-like performance and user experience consistency.

By staying informed about emerging trends and understanding the strengths and weaknesses of the available tools, developers can continue to build powerful, cross-platform applications that meet the demands of users across all platforms.

www.ingramcontent.com/pod-product-compliance
Lightning Source LLC
LaVergne TN
LVHW051435050326
832903LV00030BD/3104